Gia,
So grateful for
our Soul-and-heart
connection !
Love from
Karen

Advance Praise for *The Connected Leader*

"This innovative and inspiring book will change the reader and change the conversation around leadership. Karen has a unique and powerful way of inviting us to put connection at the center of leadership. She urges us to throw out the old leadership models and dive deep into the soul work needed to be fully human at work, and in all of life. This is a rare business book with a heartbeat."

—Susan Packard, Co-founder of HGTV and
Author of *Fully Human: 3 Steps to Grow Emotional
Fitness in Work, Leadership, and Life*

"When we think about our emotional health, we tend to think about our personal lives and neglect how it coincides with our professional lives. But our emotional health impacts not only how we show up at work but how we show up as leaders. Karen Hardwick's *The Connected Leader* is a great resource that helps us think more holistically about our leadership."

—Miles Adcox, Executive Chairman of Onsite,
Emotional Wellness Expert, Speaker

"In her beautiful book, *The Connected Leader*, author Karen Hardwick moves you to the halfway point of a joyful journey you had always dreamed of and knew was possible. The dream that awakens you each morning, yet, like a morning fog, quickly disappears as the busyness of your day begins: You can be the person you always knew you could be, the leader you had always imagined. The next half of the journey begins as you pick up this book, read it and live out its lessons. The time for hesitation is over."

—Richard Sheridan, CEO and Chief Storyteller of Menlo
Innovations, Author, *Joy, Inc.: How We Built a Workplace
People Love, and Chief Joy Officer: How Great Leaders
Elevate Human Energy and Eliminate Fear*

"I love the evolved model of *The Connected Leader* and every aspect of this insightful and inspirational book. Karen's work and thinking pushes us all forward onto a path that allows us, as leaders, to become the best version of ourselves. Karen's book is perfect for the times as we find the courage to fight the Goliaths that keep us less evolved and focused on the things that wear us down and out as leaders, and as humans. I am a big fan of Karen's human-centered approach to leadership, the stories in this book, and how she urges us all to connect deeply to ourselves and all that matters."

—Barri Rafferty, Chief Communications and
Brand Management Officer, Wells Fargo

"Working with Karen is a joy and this book captures her wisdom and the 'voice' I have come to trust over the many years we've worked together. Understanding how to grow and evolve as a leader requires that one first deeply connects with oneself. Karen's approach to leadership reinforces the notion that growth—both as an individual and a leader—requires self-awareness, the courage to be vulnerable, and a deep connectedness with others. The process detailed in *The Connected Leader* will push every leader to focus on being connected in the workplace and in one's day-to-day life."

—Rich Warren, President, WarnerMedia

"With courage, vulnerability, and clarity, Karen brings life to the value of being a connected leader. This is a must read for any leader or aspiring leader and my friend Karen lays out a new path for leadership."

—Molly Fletcher, The "Female Jerry Maguire",
Coveted Speaker, and Author of *The Energy Clock*,
Fearless at Work and *The Business of Being the Best*

"This book reflects Karen's emotional intelligence. This book, like the author, gets leaders to consciously and subconsciously become comfortable with themselves—what makes them tick, what makes them successful both professionally and personally, what makes them happy and content. Understanding these unique characteristics allows leaders to connect with others on a more human level and more confidently build relationships fueled by communication and enhanced trust. Teams with honest connections are tough to break, highly motivated, and eminently more successful. Karen has figured this out; I have taken

the journey with her and am a better person and leader for it. Read this book—it is the next best thing to sitting down with Karen."
—Bob Chitty, Senior Vice President of Corporate Investments & Transactions, Intercontinental Hotels Group

"This book is a game-changer. Karen invites us to go deep into our inner worlds and she shares much of her own story, which is heart-breaking and triumphant. She knows what it means to be rigorously self-honest, open, and willing—and the huge positive impact this authenticity can and will have on your business and career. She and I have both seen this happen and know the best leaders are embracing this genuineness. And this book is an invitation to take the path to-ward awakening and connection since life and leadership is a journey of self-discovery. Karen lays out the imperative for a new way to lead in all aspects of our personal and professional worlds: an imperative that is about empathy not ego, courage not control, mindfulness not management. So whether you are a CEO or a teacher, a full-time homemaker or an entrepreneur, this book can help you become your best, most connected, inspiring self."
—Cynthia Good, CEO and Founding Editor, Little PINK Book

"Karen's work amazes me with her perspective, courage, and emotional depth. And she brings this depth of connection to the complexities of the business world, providing a much needed challenge to leaders at senior levels which powerfully translates into far better leader aware-ness and effectiveness. This book, which is reflective of her work, is groundbreaking—spiritual and pragmatic, challenging and confirm-ing. I recommend it without hesitation."
—Larry S. Levin, PD, Author of *Top Teaming: A Roadmap for Teams Navigating the Now, the New, and the Next*

"In *The Connected Leader*, Karen Hardwick creates a blueprint for readers to courageously embrace and learn through life's experiences to become more connected leaders. Her gift of honesty and transparency reinforces the Seven Discoveries of connection to guide us through the inner work to become more connected at home and at work. This serves

as a bright light for transformational leaders—I will for sure share it with all the families, athletes, and colleagues in my orbit. Read, reflect, and follow your path to deeper connections and meaning."
—Buddy Curry, CEO, Kids and Pros, and
Former NFL player, Atlanta Falcons

"This deep, thoughtful work touches you at the core and will develop you to be the leader and person you were meant to be."
—Tonya Harris Cornileus, Ph.D., Vice
President, Human Resources, ESPN

"*The Connected Leader* is profoundly important. Karen's written a guide that is at once both practical and actionable while vividly authentic and real. Using her own broken open heart, she shows how each of us is seeking presence and connection and that the best leaders, leading from a connected soul, create the conditions for a lasting sense of belonging."
—Jerry Colonna, author, *Reboot: Leadership
and the Art of Growing Up*

"I am thankful Karen shared important insights from her life journey to help all us in these chaotic times. I read this book in two days and it is one of the best leadership books I have ever read. Her words can help each of us find our inner leader to chase slowly and say hell yes to the challenges. She weaves a powerful story with lessons using Aspens, prisms, Montana, and a Mama Elk. This is an important gift she has given our generation of leaders."
—Joe George, President, Cox Automotive Mobility

"Hardwick's inspiring message is there's a more fully human way to lead rooted in emotional, spiritual, and relational wholeness. Connected leadership is the way of the future. Highly recommended!"
—Ian Morgan Cron, author, *The Road Back to You*

THE CONNECTED LEADER

7 STRATEGIES TO EMPOWER YOUR TRUE SELF AND INSPIRE OTHERS

KAREN JOY HARDWICK,
M.DIV., MSW

Post Hill
PRESS

A POST HILL PRESS BOOK
ISBN: 978-1-64293-982-8
ISBN (eBook): 978-1-64293-983-5

The Connected Leader:
7 Strategies to Empower Your True Self and Inspire Others
© 2021 by Karen Joy Hardwick, M.Div., MSW
All Rights Reserved

Cover art by Cody Corcoran

Post Hill Press
New York • Nashville
posthillpress.com

Published in the United States of America

To my mother,
Bernice Ann Walker Benjack,
You taught me to write,
And instilled in me the joy of words.
And even though you left us way too early,
You are on every page of this book.

"Let it be for Your sake that I am loved."

~ St. Augustine

COVER ART NOTE

Aspens tend to grow in groves and benefit from a shared root system that creates new stems and growth; while they are individual trees, they are all one. Pando, an aspen clone located in Utah, spreads across 106 acres, weighs approximately thirteen million pounds, and is likely eighty thousand years old. It is the largest living organism in the world and has one interconnected root system. Aspens are also incredibly resilient; they can withstand and survive wildfires because of their strong root system and higher water content. They are so powerful against fire that often times a "candling" wildfire that burns through a forest of conifers will recede back to ground level when it hits a clump of aspen; these trees, a testimony to connection, naturally thrive after a traumatic event like logging or wildfire. Like the aspen, it is when we find courage to strengthen our roots, dig deep into our strength, and connect with others more powerfully that we are at our best, enhancing our healthy connections in every way.[1]

Foreword

Karen's approach—from which I have benefited for over a decade—
comes through with poetic, real, vulnerable, and engaging force in *The
Connected Leader*. The book truthfully, and without artifice, explores
the value of recognizing the impactful connections between work life
and home life, inner self and outer self, and between one's self and one's
team. Reading it reminded me of just how holistic, circumspect, and
true her coaching approach has struck me over the years. Exploring
and focusing on connection is one of my business imperatives as a
leader. Most other tactics, strategies, and considerations are secondary.
The truth of the power of connection forces some leaders into "training" on it over time. Karen's coaching—and this book—empowers all
of us fortunate enough to know her or to read her work to embrace
connection as an activator in business and an enhancement to our lives.

So why another leadership book? I have read many leadership
books and what feels different about this one is that its approach
is inside-out. Instead of telling stories of corporate triumphs which
were analyzed, dissected, and then formulated into a leadership philosophy, Karen starts with the truth about ourselves. Our fears. Our
senses of loneliness. Our self-inflicted wounds and our ever-surprising
strengths. She starts from this precious, inner place by telling stories
about her own wonderful, tragic, triumphant up-and-down life. Her
vulnerability and willingness to point to her own history means that
no anecdote rings falsely, no story feels off point, and no exemplar
appears forced.

The same holds true and she journeys from the inside to the
outside. The stories of her coaching and clients provide compelling
meaning and generate understanding. The architecture of her Seven

Strategies of Connection are action-oriented, self-reinforcing, and easily understood. And because again, it starts with what is inside of all of us, what reads like a revolution on the page feels like common sense on reflection. But common sense on the street corner, in the C-Suite to the seat of government is in too short supply these days. Connections by their nature can bridge the divides in our world, whether they be between conservative and liberal, rural and urban, or any of the other artifices of separations all only of our own making.

The Strategies of Connection that Karen espouses ring true for all parts of a human being's life, not just leading. So, I think it would be incomplete to call this a leadership book. Again, Karen crosses boundaries between the medical and the spiritual, biography and polemic, corporate strategy and individual addiction, work and family, our inner and outer lives, organizational health and personal wellness—you name it. A "Leadership Philosophy"? Try "Life Philosophy."

—Paul Snyder
Executive Vice President, Stewardship
Tillamook

August 2021

Acknowledgments

I am an acknowledgment junkie. The first thing I do when I open a book is read the acknowledgments; I can tell so much about an author's heart and soul by reading this glimpse into their life. It is a tough task: to write acknowledgments, and I do not do so lightly. Gratitude is a radical act, and I am radically grateful for so very many.

So many people are walking me home, connecting deeply with me, and, as a result, helping me to step into my true self. Thank you to all of you for helping me to see that the work of a lifetime is for me to connect to myself, be Karen, and let God be God.

To my clients: the individual executives, teams, and entire organizations. You know who you are. Our work is sacred. Confidential. So while I would love to thank you by name, I cannot. Please remember how I am your student. I am unendingly grateful for all you teach me to and for the openness and vulnerability with which you share yourself with me.

To all the authors whose books line my shelves, weigh down my nightstand, and fill my bags when I travel…. Thank you! Your words have endlessly nourished me. Much gratitude to the following: Elizabeth Lesser, Rosamund Stone Zander and Benjamin Zander, Shauna Niequist, Mark Nepo, Daniel J. Siegel, Jon Kabat-Zinn, Melody Beattie, Richard Rohr, Thomas Keating, Mary Oliver, Krissy Pozatek, Harriet Goldhor Lerner, Parker Palmer, Bob Goff, and Tara Brach to name only several that inspire me. And to Anne Lamott, who said, "You own everything that happened to you. Tell your stories. If people wanted you to write warmly about them, they should have behaved better." Thanks and wow!

To Katelyn Murphy-McCarthy, who read a version of this with a poet's eye and a critic's encouragement. I thank you. Much of what you suggested was incorporated. I am tremendously appreciative for the effort and energy you generously spent with my words.

To the shining lights, Sydney Welch and Sophie Lobuglio, who help me stir the oatmeal metaphorically, tend to clients, keep things going when I am consumed by writing and do all the marketing kinds of stuff someone like me needs to do, thank you! Your boundless energy, wickedly bright intelligence, and devotion humble me.

To Justin Spizman, the most patient of all book architects/editors who told me a long time ago that I had a powerful voice that needed to be shared. Thank you for working with such steadfastness on this project, for accepting how life's detours made this book better, and for your ability to call me on my stuff. No one should write a book without your counsel, input, and wisdom. You rock. I trust you.

Thank you to the team at BookStar PR. A rousing shout-out to Jim Knight and Brant Menswar, expert guides and rock stars. A million thank yous for your expertise, tireless encouragement, ma p-holding-trail-blazing-walk-this-way encouragement. We have each been through our own valley through this process and never once did you not show up with open-hearted connection and invaluable counsel.

Thanks to John Willig, my literary agent and consummate cheerleader. Thank you for taking a chance on this first-time author and for holding the light steady, ensuring that my work would find a home. And it did, thanks to your belief in me, our work together, and the power of connection. You are decidedly the best.

To Scott and Abbey—once someone joins my team, it is kind of a hold-on-and-strap-yourself-in lifelong-journey. I am sure you have realized that by now. For your wise counsel mixed with compassion, generosity, and kindness, I am forever grateful.

To Gary Figiel, MD and Valerie Fanning, your expertise and warm-hearted insights shone a light on the path I walked with my husband. Your steady clinical care and compassionate support held me up during the toughest, most intensely stressful times. You are truly heroes.

To my team at Post Hill for guiding me through this publication process. Thank you to Debra Englander for your wise counsel, discernment, and support. And to the whole team; I am grateful that this expertise and keen insight made my writing and voice better and clearer. This has been such a joyful process and my gratitude to: Heather King, Devon Brown, Dev Murphy, Brandon Rospond, and Rachel Hoge.

To the Ranches at Belt Creek for creating a place that no one ever wants to leave. God provided the raw material and you all show up delivering on His promise, every day. Thank you to Brett and Mark for living connected leadership. Brett, for your big heart and for welcoming us to the big skies with such generosity and spirit. To Mark, for your humility and discipleship as you serve lovingly and intentionally. Here's to Grace and Grit, two things you two embody every day.

To Chad and Jessica, who dragged me kickin' and screaming into the world of podcasts, headphones, and the recording world. I have been blessed by your empathy, your expertise, and your ability to make all things podcast fun. I will definitely save you a seat at any table of my mine. Your expertise is matched only by your big-hearted, loving ways.

To Hasani, you helped me move into being a thought leader by stepping into my gifts; I know it is a tough job and that I am not easy. I am grateful for your strategic brilliance and your marketing savvy. Thank you for leading with your story and encouraging me to tell mine in all of its messiness.

To Molly Fletcher, my true game changer friend. Your humility is only bested by your generosity of heart and spirit. Since you have been referred to as the female Jerry Maguire, I just have to say it: "You had me at hello." I am continually grateful for your loving presence.

To Susan Packard, my fellow journeyer on the path of progress, not perfection. From the moment we chatted, I wanted to have you in my circle; and now that I do, I am lifted up by how fully human you are. Thank you for your desire to connect in sustaining ways.

To Ian Morgan Cron. Your work has added much richness to my work, self-discovery, and commitment to walking this path one day at a time. Working closely with you and collaborating on leadership initiatives is sheer magic. And thanks to *The Road Back to You*, this Enneagram Two is forever doubling down on the importance of healing in solitude.

To my teachers and guides—Judith Stark, you were the first woman I ever knew personally who lives the life she chooses and makes it a damn inspiring one; meeting you on my first day of undergraduate life at Seton Hall changed me and here we are, decades later, friends and fellow believers in how important it is to stay away from the "avoidable suffering syndrome". Helen Graham—you brought me into your circle and taught me to welcome healing hands and embrace vulnerability. Gay Haley—we have shared such adventures, and most people would never believe the paths we have walked and the miracles we have witnessed; thank you for never wavering in your wisdom-dispensing guidance and unmatched expertise. Nick Firaldi—thank you for helping me break through in the wilderness and be the change I needed to be; your voice still fills my kitchen and heart. Lucinda Patterson and Laura Wolff—you both tied together the body, soul, and heart for me in perfect harmony and healing, freeing my energy to be all it can be. To Nicole Rubin—my guide through one hell of a breaking-wide-open; you encouraged me to see love in bloom. To Neale Lundgren, for holding steady and bringing the attention back to my soul-work.

To Luke, who wears a cape and handles the details so the lights can stay on. I don't know how you have put up with my zany disorganization all these years, but I am beyond-words appreciative that you have, and that you have done it all with such belief in me. I know I am a full-time job and that you deserve sainthood.

To those of us who meet in church basements, clubhouse rooms, and anywhere two or more of us are gathered, you are the tribe that fuels my courage, serenity, and wisdom. And especially to the badass warrior moms with whom I would enter into any battle, any time; we have been brought to our knees, and we do rise, empowered and powerless.

To the young people who fill my home, surround my table, and teach me what true connection really is: you are the greatest miracles. I will make blueberry puff for you 'til the end of my days and keep a light on for you always.

To Griffin. We keep the vigil.

To Scott. You are one steadfast, faithful friend whose ability to check on me must be divinely inspired, because it is always perfectly timed. Thank you for your empathy and loving understanding. Your momma would be so proud of the man you are.

To Vince for teaching me more about having a Higher Power than I ever thought possible; I am down-to-my-bones grateful that I am one of the ones who get to benefit from your journey, love, and endless hope. And to Connie, a beautiful friend inside and out, whose quiet soulful way is calming and inspiring.

To my sisters-in-law Debbie and Cindy, who stand in the gap next to me. Thank you for welcoming me into your circle and for never wavering in your support. Debbie—I have always been touched by your prayerful, kind gestures. And Cindy—we have shared the details of our brutal journeys with hearts wide open and forever changed; thank you for being such a fierce warrior and loving, truth-telling defender.

For my brothers-in-law Scott and Jimmy. For Scott—no longer with us—whose welcoming love still watches over us from above. And for Jimmy: your steadfastness is a source of quiet comfort. Thank you for always reminding me about the power found when we fall on our knees.

To Billy and Judy: what can I say? You are my rocks in a swirling stream and were my husband's most faithful, lifelong friends. Thank you for riding shotgun with us every day, through everything, and having my back without question, because you know my heart. I will never be able to thank you enough.

For my superhero girlfriends who, in my eyes, leap tall buildings in a single bound, please know that you hold up the world for me. This is not a do-it-yourself life, and you are my emotional, spiritual, and laugh-'til-it-hurts-let's-get-some-food people.

For Elaine whose history with me is marked by steadfastness, faithful love, and the living Christ; thank you for your decades-long belief in me.

For Grace, who over the seasons of our lives and miles offers healing insights, thank you for being true connection.

To Kelly, sweet and open companion who would do anything, arrange any party, run any errand, show up anywhere and for anything. Your heart and faith are matched only by your energy. To Catherine, my ride-or-die shotgun-rider and baked-macaroni-and-cheese-out-o f-the-pan-sharer. You helped me to drop the rock and pick up courage, serenity, and wisdom. Endlessly grateful. You know why. Beth, thank you for the 6 a.m. calls, the deep-into-my-soul understanding, and grace-filled authenticity, along with simply, faithfully keeping watch. I am forever with you and you with me; we are the luckiest. KT, you crack me up, show up (everywhere and every time I need you), and lift me up with your thoughtfulness and full-out loving humanness. So many years behind us and in front of us. To Meredith, you know there are no words, right? How you put up with my nutty intensity is beyond me, but when you showed up on our doorstep fifteen years ago not knowing what you were signing up for, you changed my life. Every day since then, your friendship is a reminder that God is not worried. What would I do without you? I don't want to know.

To my first cousins, Debbie, Thomas, Jim, John, and Ed. You were there at the beginning and witnessed firsthand all the stuff at number 44 that made us who we are today; my deep connection to you remains, across the miles and decades. I grew up thinking you were the most special and magical people, and I still think that. My love for you is reserved for people who have been there every fabulous, heartbreaking step of the way, and with whom I grew up on a steady diet of stuffed cabbage and icebox cake.

To Claire, my sister-in-law, a nourisher of the land, and as a result, many a body. Thank you for the many decades of growing our bond stronger and for sharing your three boys with me throughout many a season; being an aunt gave me the courage to step off the cliff into motherhood, and your generosity with your sons was a magical part of that. We have taught each other a lot. Thank you for all of it. Some of my most amazing times have been spent in a kitchen or around a table with you.

To my siblings. My deepest roots. My fiercest histories. Jane Marie, from our earliest days you have given me much grist for the mill. It is because of your gifts to me that I can step boldly into my gifts. David John, I can do this thing called life because, regardless of its messiness, you are there, evolving with me, and rooting for me without fail. This world needs more men like you: faithful, mindful, soulful. No one but you has been with me every messy, zany, what-the-hell, loving step of the way. Lucky you…it has been some journey and I am down-to-my-bones grateful for you.

To Greg, my very own desperado and jukebox who ran the good race. I believed you when you said I was the love of your life and I made one helluva choice when I married you. Because of you and what I surrendered to, I doubled down on my courage, empathy, and boundary-making to stay open and create sacred space for you, for us, and for our son. You got your heart's desire; I walked you Home and was privileged beyond measure to do so.

To Matthew, my most honest feedback giver, powerful alchemist, and greatest miracle. You were born to me, yet it was you who renewed my life. You are God's present of a lifetime. You leave me speechless (which is really hard to do!) as I witness your strength, courage, resilience, and willingness to be honest in a way that literally restores sanity and enhances life. I stand by you, forever, and love you to the moon and back. Straight up, my love!

To God the Father, God the Son, and God the Holy Spirit. It is because of You, and despite me, that I chase slow, dig deep, and rise up one day at a time. To You be all the glory.

Contents

Introduction

"What is success? It is being able to go to bed
each night with your soul at peace."
—*Paulo Coelho*

Though I honed the Connected Leader philosophy through what I learned from my clients, in fact, it took seed in my childhood. Decades passed before I realized this.

My mother was diagnosed with a terminal illness when I was ten, the oldest of three. At that age, I became an adult, totally unprepared to be one yet totally willing if it would save her. This one sentence captures a major part of my lifelong baggage, heavy enough to need a forklift and in desperate need of a major miracle. With each passing year between her diagnosis and death, Mom became increasingly isolated and fearful. She was mostly afraid to leave her three young children, as she was the only adult in the household capable of raising us.

As her fear grew, she became so focused on not dying, she forgot to live. She did not know how to reach out from her own terror and get support; only because of her strong-willed love and devotion to us kids did she live as long as she did. In the midst of her fearful darkness, she managed to teach us kindness and empathy; she was compassionate and generous with her heart. She also managed to teach us how to be afraid of public toilet seats and anything that smacked of spontaneous fun. We lived on high alert at all times.

Yet, through these hellacious years, we soldiered through emotional and spiritual complexities. Mom struggled mightily with acknowledging her children's and her own layered emotions. As if her physical illness was not enough, mental illness was galloping behind it at a brisk pace. In fact, we were all just skating ahead of the cracks as the intergenerational legacy of addiction and abuse beat the drum of insanity, people-pleasing, and denial. It was quite the three-strikes-and-you-are-out scenario, but we were good soldiers often marching around the living room singing "Onward, Christian Soldiers" (we actually did this). It was quite zany, if not downright heartbreaking: singing at the top of our lungs while much was crumbling around us, but we did not know what we did not know. We kids were earnest, but we had nowhere to go with our humanness. That was the problem.

We did not have a safe place to explore the catastrophe of our feelings. At home, Mom was consumed with her terror and focused on crazy details she could control like marking up our homework (before we handed it in to our teachers). In her world, knowing the difference between a colon and a semi-colon would save us and make life easier.

In addition to being good little soldiers at home, church was yet another place for us to demonstrate everything was A-OK as we attended choir practice, youth group, and all things potluck. And of course, school was another perfect place for us to consistently prove, without a shadow of a doubt, that we were truly special and not falling apart from the inside out. We shone with rule-abiding behavior and stellar report cards, extracurricular activities, and for my brother athleticism good enough to earn a college scholarship.

And even though there was much to recover from on a daily basis, Mom, who was a survivor of tremendous trauma, did open her heart as well as she could, along with her Bible. We witnessed Mom searching through winter coat pockets in the hope she would find enough change to buy milk. We watched while she said nothing to address all the nuttiness going on around us. We witnessed her anxiety attacks triggered by her concern that she had hurt someone's feelings at a PTA meeting knowing full well she probably did not even open her mouth. I came home complaining of being bullied in junior high, and neither she or my Dad could muster the strength to put themselves out there and protect me. These were just a few things we were all processing, recovering from, and burying on a daily basis. There were others.

On the other hand, because we human beings are complex, Mom had many wonderful, life-giving strengths. She was a world-class listener, providing sacred space to us, our cousins, and a myriad of friends; I still have people reaching out to me to tell me what a loving difference she made in their lives. Our small, shabby living room was my favorite place to be, sitting with her, having our friends join in our conversations, listening to her stories, watching her pray for others, and witnessing how she helped others feel heard.

And so it was both as it can be for many of us: Mom was amazingly present in some ways and amazingly shut down in others. She was open about some of her story, like what it was like to have an alcoholic father, an abused mother, and to marry—at the age of eighteen—a man who emotionally and physically tortured her and then who was killed by a train when she was twenty-one. She wrote short stories about how her mother, aunt, sister, and cousins were nourished by The Church of St. Luke in the Fields in the heart of Greenwich Village: how liturgy and summers at church camp were literally her saving grace. She spoke about how her high school teachers urged her to go on to college and become a writer because she was just so darn talented and bright; but instead, she married the handsome, charming boy who held her hostage and beat her.

She told her stories as a cautionary tale, hoping their warnings would be absorbed. She wanted others to feel comfortable sharing their stories and process their struggles; she created the space for many to do so.

Yet, there were these little sticking points about which we hardly spoke. How the emotional impact of addiction swirled around in our lives courtesy of my grandfathers' alcoholism, abuse, and damage perpetrated on my mother and father. How my mother stiffened each time my father drank his daily beer, which he found money to buy when we had no money for other things, like enough food. How my father's emotional abuse was a regular dinner guest and his physical abuse was something I learned to say "that did not hurt" to. And how my father was not able to stand up to his mother who lived with us, filled our house with passive-aggressive nonsense, and relentlessly shamed my mother. Oh yes…and there was the fact that mom, the center of it all for me, was dying.

My two younger siblings and I had few coping tools, so we worked harder, prayed harder, and stuck together harder, somehow hoping that if we did manage everything perfectly, she would live. Mom was our glue, and when she died, it fell apart. Each of us, overwhelmed with the weight of our grief, struggled to find our way. And each of us have a different perspective on those years depending on our role in the family, how we were treated by our parents, what was expected of us, and what we carried, as a result.

Through the decades since my mother passed, I have been held up by loving people who taught me to build on my strengths and connect consciously, listen deeply, exhibit empathy, celebrate curiosity, demonstrate accountability, navigate chaos comfortably, and walk with confidence: the seven strategies of what I now call the Connected Leader philosophy. This way of life is designed to deepen connection. This way of life creates the path through the collective heartbreak and uncertainty we find in this life; it also helps us to tap into the grace, joy, and gratitude that humbles and inspires us. This way of life functions as a lighthouse calling us to the safe harbor of our true selves.

These seven attributes create connection by guiding us through the messy process of enhancing emotional wholeness, spiritual strength, relational wellbeing, and mental health: the mainstays of sustainable leadership in work and life. They encourage us to chase slow, dig deep, and rise up. They walk us home to ourselves, which is the path to God and to others. Healthy connection is a cyclical, cumulative, synergistic process between self, the divine, and others.

Interestingly, these seven attributes are the very things I needed when my mother was dying; I did not have consistent enough access to them, although they were visible on the horizon and I experienced glimpses of them. Today, they are the qualities I have anchored myself in with the help of my guides, the power of the twelve steps, my loved ones and dear friends, and my clients.

I hope to teach them to you, too.

The Path to a New Leadership

This is not a book about leadership, in the traditional sense. Spare us from another leadership model that promises a one-size-fits-all leadership solution. This is a "quality of life and self-discovery" book meant to expand the definition of who a leader is, explore how leaders are on a spiritual and emotional journey, and discuss how Connected Leaders are needed even more these days at work and in life.

We don't need another leadership paradigm; we need our stories and truest selves. We need to dig deep into self-discovery and use what we find there to uncover our purpose—our most authentic way of living—and form relationships in healthy, sustainable, and energizing ways. We need this balm of interrelatedness to help us become unstuck from the distractions and pain that limit our true potential.

As leaders at work (and in life), let's back away from the MBA style of leadership—process, models, checklists—and run toward the connecting way of leadership based on being fully human, hopeful, resilient, and open. Let's lay down our ego-driven hustle for approval and lean into our intentional vulnerability, accepting our life story. We need to embark on self-exploration, viewing our lives as archeological digs that hold lessons and wounds that need to be excavated and examined in the light of day; these are the treasures that hold the key to us leading and living from a place of mystery and authenticity, honesty and willingness.

Though we are wired to connect, we need a primer to show us how. It is not enough to say we are wired to connect. It is not sufficient to say connection is the antidote and the opposite of all things that separate us from ourselves, like addiction and emotional or relational dishonesty. This book is designed to shine light on how to nourish healthy connections. This book was created to prompt deep reflection, because human beings need self-reflection and self-discovery to ground ourselves in our center, the place from which an empowering, healthy, and inspiring life flows. If we do not learn how to do this, how are we to complete the mission with which we are entrusted: our purpose, our reason for being here in human school?

We reside in an interconnected world filled with joy and magic, overwhelm and heartbreak. Even with the benefits of modern-day life, we have challenges that can feel insurmountable, worrisome, and disconnecting. We sometimes create stress for ourselves (shocking, yes) while the world does its part to add to the chaos: at the time of writing, we are struggling through a global COVID pandemic, an uptick in violence across the board, and an increase in mental health challenges.

All the while, decisions are being made by many—in business, politics, and other positions of influence—who are sociopathic, power-hungry, wounded, and highly manipulative. How different it would be if more of our influential leaders nourished an inner life and were involved in a deeply healing spiritual and emotional process that would help them examine their unresolved hurts, losses, fears, and defense mechanisms.

We are a culture that confuses busyness with purpose. Social media with connection. Instagram scrolling with therapy and spiritual direction. Wealth with wellbeing. And self-obsession with vulnerability.

To put it simply, we have not learned—collectively—how to be fully human, connected, honest, and open enough. We are too busy blaming, shaming, and diffusing. We have normalized the craziness around us and within us, and we believe the solution is in "fixing" the outward symptoms instead of turning within to heal our wounds and fears.

We are focused on what is wrong outside of ourselves instead of addressing how we normalize and ignore our internal defects, the very things that create the dysfunction in our work cultures, families, and communities. And sometimes, we even enhance our internal defects like fear and self-righteousness by leveraging them for entertainment:

gossiping about others, pointing fingers, threatening others so they comply. This hyper-focus, on the outside instead of the inside, makes it easier for those in charge to play us like pawns on a chessboard as the emphasis becomes disconnection and differences; we continue to ignore the fact that what is wrong in our society is fueled by our human brokenness, trauma, and pain.

The disconnection and inner trauma, which we all have to some degree, is the true gateway drug—it pushes many of us humans to find a fix that will numb the pain. It encourages us to use the things that foster even more disconnection, fear, and woundedness. When emotional stress becomes unbearable, hijacks our self-worth, and poisons our thinking, this trauma can be the gateway that ushers us into a world of addiction (which has many forms) in an attempt to alleviate our suffering. It is heartbreaking.

While we are wired to connect, these manifestations of disconnection exist because fear, a pandemic in its own right, grows faster than a virus. Disconnection in the workplace can mirror disconnection in life. Disengaged leaders often suffer from also being disengaged spouses, friends, and parents; and above all else, they are most disconnected from themselves.

We cannot connect with anyone in sustainable, healthy ways unless we connect with ourselves in meaningful, honest ways. Please read that again, because that is critical and a mainstay of this book. We cannot lead or engage anyone until we accept what we need to about ourselves: the shadowy, flawed sides and the magical, loving sides.

When people are not connected to their true self and an abiding sense of purpose, it is more difficult for them to experience a sense of strength, an infusion of resilience, an elevation in wellbeing, or their part in the bigger picture. They are unable to lead with the blended mind, heart, and soul required of a Connected Leader.

We need Connected Leaders in every part of our daily lives—people who connect with themselves, understand and transform the fears and flaws holding them back, awaken to their true self, learn how truly whole and holy they are, and lead intentionally to inspire others. Yet this is a daunting task in a time of relentless work demands, increasing client needs, marketplace chaos, global violence and viruses, proliferating addictions along with depression and anxiety, and the push-pull swipe-left of daily lives.

For that reason, we need more people to run toward connection like golden retrievers run toward the ball—joyfully, enthusiastically— and to understand what it really is, how to deepen it, and how to encourage it in as many people as possible...starting with themselves.

The seven strategies laid out in this book foster and nurture connection so we don't just relegate the word "connection" to the category of buzzword or concept.

It is the antidote, at work and home, for those of us interested in leadership as a way of life. This fully human approach begins with the inside work. The work we might not want to do. The work that makes spreadsheets, board meetings, and reorgs look like child's play. The work that is the most courageous, rewarding, and empowering: the work that allows us to use the power of our story to connect with others.

Connection creates a true sense of empowerment which is most assuredly what we need more of in the workplace, but it is not something that spontaneously happens because we will it to happen:

> *Empowerment, fueled by connection, is present when leaders create a psychologically safe environment in which their people can thrive, take risks, and depend on a leader showing up in consistently, healthy ways. Empowerment allows people to step into their gifts and learn from their mistakes. It is the energy which teaches them to believe in themselves.*
>
> *It occurs when a leader believes in the importance of people finding their own wisdom. It thrives when people are encouraged to embark on a journey of self-discovery, understand clear rules of engagement and performance standards,*

*and trust their leader has their back while also holding
boundaries firm.*

*The behaviors that contribute to empowerment can be
taught, coached, and encouraged, because they flow from
and contribute to a behavioral model that enhances our
neurobiological need for connection, emotional wholeness,
relational wellbeing, spiritual strength, and mental health.*

*Empowerment means we are owning the power found in
our story to create a collective understanding, a rising up,
a healing and hope.*

My story includes the screened porch that sits on the back of our
home, overlooking the bamboo and the swimming pool. During the
long, slow months of a humid Southern spring, summer, and fall, we
pretty much live out there. Meals. Coffee. Conversation. The porch
is made even better when, from the comfort of welcoming wicker
and plush pillows, we have a front row seat to a thick and thunderous
rainstorm.

Our porch is not just a porch. It is a sanctuary, a sacred place. It is
a glass-of-tea and a take-your-shoes-off-place.

I have entertained corporate clients on the porch. It is often filled
with young adults draped over the chairs as they eat and talk and
share the secrets of growing up. I often sit out there, in solitude or
with my tribe.

I have felt disconnection, the anti-porch, which is why I now
run to connection as hard as I can. There is no porch during the
cunning and baffling nights. Disconnection can feel like shame and
soul-sucking denial, isolation and depleting self-blame. Disconnection
is very anti-porch. It is about control, because disconnection tells us
this lie: if the rules are rigid enough and we are powerful enough, no
danger can destroy what we love the fiercest or want the most.

Yet, during this season of overwhelm exacerbated by a global
pandemic and its associated collective grief, the elixir is all things

porch-like: being with my tribe, trusting our deepest truths, talking about the ghosts that still haunt, and eating as much bacon and chocolate as we can.

Last night, as the candles flickered and the rain fell, my son, Matthew, and I sat on the porch. The phone rang. Not unexpected. He took the call, and I could hear the familiar tone and words he often uses. He then looked at me after hanging up, and we both knew he had to leave to be with whoever it was that was on the other end of the phone.

For you see, connection is designed to be taken on the road beyond the porch, into our homes, workplaces, and souls.

Connection gives us the grace and grit to unleash our potential and endure the challenge of our daily mess. The grueling pressures and stressors of this moment, defined by the pandemic and all that it has uncovered, are creating a leadership movement that needs connection as its mascot. The kind of connection that transforms us, our workplaces, and our relationships while shining light on our larger purpose. The kind of recalibration that is creating the Connection Era: a time when more people are recognizing that a soulful and mindful approach to leadership is what will transform and not just inform.

Most leaders agree our connection currency is at an all-time low. But what caused our connection bankruptcy? Was it the pandemic? The associated pressures? Not likely, because if you look at workplaces and our collective mental health before this moment in time, emotional and spiritual angst was running rampant while often denied and normalized. The usual suspects—depression, anxiety, and addiction—have been around for a long time.

In short, the pandemic hasn't caused our condition. It has shed light on it. It has made it more obvious that leaders are experiencing a human being crisis that is ushering us into where we need to go: the Connection Era. Leaders are no longer expected to just enhance the bottom line; many are now being given the sacred duty of spiritually awakening, emotionally healing, and courageously leading from a platform of inclusion, wholeness, and connection. This, along with their fiduciary and operational responsibilities, elevates the stakes substantially.

This isn't a kumbaya. This is not a "soft" skill. It's an essential ingredient that fuels leaders' ability to move people and achieve outcomes. Whether you're a corporate leader, change champion in the community, or full-time-parent, the battle cry of our people, those entrusted to us, is clear. People want leaders who have the self-awareness to connect entire organizations, systems, and movements around the things that make us human, honest, and whole.

Connection as a Superpower

The ability to deepen connection lies in awakening to self-discovery. Period. That is why self-discovery is so important.

Everything that matters rests on the realization that this life is an inside job: our spiritual, relational, emotional, mental, and physical wellbeing hinges wildly on our ability to accept the full catastrophe of who we are. And if we don't, connection is compromised as is our ability to lead; they are inextricably linked.

We connect by being brave in the most courageous ways: by wrestling with our fears, surrendering to win, accepting our mistakes, celebrating our strengths, stepping out of entrenched patterns that keep us stuck, and embracing our vulnerabilities. It is what we do in the rooms of church basements as we accept our powerlessness. It is what we do when we come to someone we love, hands and heart open, saying, "I am truly sorry. Can we talk? This is how I am going to change." It is what we do when we tell our executive team that we are embarking on a coaching process that will contribute to an organizational, cultural transformation.

It is about reinforcing an emotionally wise mind that understands mistakes are not life sentences but lessons; I am saying this as someone whose mistakes have been costly. It means accepting that grief is not something to work through but an experience to incorporate into our souls; I am saying this as someone whose grief has been heavy. As we embrace our mistakes and absorb our grief, we come to understand two points of wisdom: everything belongs and, our resilience is a function of our connection to ourselves, others, and God's grace.

So much of turning toward this wisdom hinges on our ability to chase slow. Chasing slow is like weightlifting for the soul. It is a mindset and heartset that reminds us to be in the moment, welcome solitude and stillness, find joy in simple pleasures, move gently with the flow, and forgive ourselves when we do none of that. It means not agonizing over what would make a project an "A+" when a "B" works fine, even a "C." My editor knows firsthand how often I torment myself with perfection instead of celebrating progress. And my team has seen me, far too many times, back away from an opportunity because I wonder, "What could I possibly have to offer?"

Chasing slow means there is value in creating a space to quiet our racing thoughts, our inner critic, and our push to constantly perform. Chasing slow means recognizing that rest is a damn good strategy: it allows us to know our soul—which is not a whole lot of fun, a lot of the time. Chasing slow encourages us to lead from the inside out instead of distracting ourselves with outside solutions; it is only by connecting with ourselves that we can inspire others. As Leo Tolstoy said, "Everyone thinks of changing the world, but no one thinks of changing himself."[2]

When we chase slow, we cry uncle and realize no amount of activism or protesting will heal our insides. Chasing slow allows us to accept that true transformation starts at home, deep within.

Along with chasing slow, Connected Leaders develop an emotionally, spiritually, and mentally healthy approach to leadership in life and at work:

- *Emotionally healthy* people can identify, accept, and regulate their emotions so that emotions don't hijack them; we are so much more than our feelings, yet they are important messengers for us. Emotionally whole people do not use emotions to browbeat, threaten, or shame themselves or others. It does not mean they do not feel life's ups and downs; it does mean they acknowledge the feeling, let it sink in, come to grips with it, and move on. They are emotionally agile, not perfect. They understand that emotions, like rain clouds, are impermanent. And sometimes—just sometimes—they have to take a massive timeout, sit with why they are feeling the way they are, and ask themselves what else might be going on underneath the surface. Emotionally whole people are mindful about choosing a constructive response—not perfectly, but intentionally, and if they can't, they do their livin' best to hit the pause button and seek guidance from others who, in that moment, may be sane when they are not. They navigate relationship dynamics with a wisdom that comes from a well of introspection and self-compassion.

- *Spiritually healthy* people experience a oneness with the larger world, recognizing we are more similar than different, more connected than separate, and that every moment is an opportunity to create sacred space. This deep sense of connection flows from believing there is One from whom our being and purpose flow, and that we are in relationship with this One. Some people call this God, others Love, Buddha, or a Higher Power; whatever the name, it restores us to sanity. For me, the One is God the Trinity. Jesus is my guy; He rides shotgun with me, although sometimes I imagine Him rolling His eyes and wondering why He even got in the car with me. It has been a wild ride. And yet, while Jesus is my guy, I get He is not everyone's. Spiritually strong folks recognize that the more we awaken, the less we know. They understand true freedom lies in embracing how often they have strayed and fallen down. And spiritual fitness allows folks to surrender and let God be God. I struggled with this for most of my life. I sometimes still crave control, misguided soul that I am. I imagine God is relieved when I (we) remember that spirituality is for people who have raised hell, created hell, and walked through hell. As someone whose walk was more of a crawl, I remind myself of this every day.

- *Mentally healthy* people recognize the power inherent in taking care of their mental wellbeing much the same way people care for their physical bodies. They engage in proactive practices like meditation, exercise, and relaxation rituals that prepare them to better handle the times when they are out of gas. Like an athlete practices drill after drill to develop muscle memory on which they can depend when it is time to perform, mentally healthy people develop the same kind of "mental memory." This acts like a reflex in the nanosecond that a healthy response is required during an intense situation. They recognize their stress triggers and seek support from others before they even need it. They are not free from battles with depression, anxiety, and addiction; they name their inner demons, depower them by accepting them and looking them in the eye, and make peace with them in nourishing ways. Some of us have had lots and lots of practice.

Please do not get me wrong. This is not about being evolved, done, or better. Connection is rooted in ongoing, hour by hour rigorous self-honesty and humility. People who prioritize being emotionally, spiritually, and mentally healthy would be the first to admit they still have crazy moments and even days. Yet, they realize that numbing or tapping out by turning to self-destructive behaviors is not helpful and that self-compassion is a gamechanger. They also realize that feeling crazy and acting crazy are two different things, and it is best to do all they can to not act out their craziness.

When the board meeting tanks, the divorce papers are served, the competitor wins, or the beloved child is sinking faster than a life vest can be found, those who live from a place of emotional and spiritual fitness integrate what is breaking them wide open into their life story. They might not do this right away because, after all, they are painfully human, need time to sort through their complex emotions, and maybe just have a meltdown or two. Yet they grow from life's fickleness and pain instead of fighting it. They know that when they show up openhearted, look the terrifying things in the eye, and lean into their inner well of wisdom, they will not be shaken. Stirred perhaps, but not shaken.

Who Is a Leader?

Leadership. It's a word we throw around. Those who lead from a place of connection act tirelessly as a bright lantern, guiding their followers through the often dimly lit caves of business, relationships, and myriad challenges. The requirements of leadership are substantial and call for those leading from the front to be conscious, mindful, and aware of all that can occur in the dimly lit places and shine in the well-lit moments.

It is how a leader navigates all of it that matters: the dark wilderness and the lighted paths. And that has nothing to do with one's title at work and more to do with how one holds themselves and interacts with others.

In nearly every aspect of our lives, the world cries out for people who can connect with themselves, navigate changing and often confusing landscapes, and thrive as they point the way for others. Whether it is on the construction site, in the locker room, in basement meeting rooms of churches, or in the C-suite, we need more leaders who can show others the way. Great leaders courageously show up with a sense of self-awareness and vulnerability so that those around them are inspired to also be brave, create safe spaces, and grow into wholeness.

My chief of staff and close friend, Meredith, has been with me since she walked in fifteen years ago to be my son's nanny. Poor thing. She had no idea what she was signing up for: dealing with my neurotic, over-the-top, big-hearted life. She now knows that once people enter my orbit and do so lovingly, it is a lifelong contract. My son was so little then, and though he outgrew the need for a nanny many, many years ago I, alas, did not. Meredith is the one I turn to for advice and counsel on life, parenting, and growing my business. I hardly make a move without getting her to weigh in with her practical advice and no-nonsense guidance. It helps that she knows me, inside and out, and does not run for the hills. (Some folks are braver than others.) Her leadership is a function not of title but of wisdom, influence, and trust. It flows from her self-acceptance. She serves yet has amazingly clear boundaries. She is a superhero who does not try to be one, but who is because she knows and honors herself. And while I might sign her paycheck, without a mistake, it is her leading me most days.

Those qualities often remain buried inside each of us. It is much more acceptable to walk into the work environment with chins held high to appear certain and fearless. It is more common to build walls at home to protect ourselves from disappointment, pain, and our own wounds. We push vulnerability aside, even when we are with people who can be trusted, deciding it is just not a high priority or an effective skill, or wondering if it might leave us too exposed.

And so, as tides change within our companies, homes, and communities, becoming someone who can navigate the chaos and noise with peace and wisdom is critical. If you don't find the right vessel to help you weather the storm, you might go through life rudderless.

One Martin Luther King, Jr. weekend, a group of high school boys sat around our kitchen table after they had made the rounds to places like Morehouse College, Martin Luther King, Jr. National Historic Park, and the Civil Rights Walk of Fame. They were visiting Atlanta from my son's boarding school, and they were on a weekend-long adventure exploring all things Civil Rights. Facilitated by two faculty members over a brunch big enough to feed a small village, they had a conversation about race, friendship, and creating change in the world. While they were consuming copious amounts of food, I listened to their stories and began to see them as torch bearers through the darkness.

Here's why. I witnessed a conversation ripe with self-reflection and honesty. They talked about the microaggressions they unknowingly directed toward themselves and others. (I loved the fact that they included the damage they did to themselves. It showed real emotional awareness.) They spoke about the need to find practical ways to enhance their emotional and social intelligence. They were a diverse group of high school boys from different backgrounds and races; they shared experiences of racism they had witnessed, dished out, and endured. There were even more stories of grace, resilience, and love in the face of failures and rejection. They were wise, self-aware, and poetic—athletes, artists, and academics among them.

Who were these evolving souls, minds, and hearts who—despite the fact that their frontal cortexes were still not connected—managed to connect consciously? And in such a heart-stopping, authentic way.

If the boys in my home that morning become leaders who will sit around boardroom tables, kitchen tables, negotiating tables, and tables found in places of worship, we are okay.

It's Not about the Title

The truth: leadership has no barriers and no boundaries. Leadership is found in all parts of life. Look around you. Who inspires you? Who helps you see challenges as invitations to grow? Who encourages you to acknowledge and heal your shadowy parts? Who creates a sacred space so you can talk openly and just be? Consider who, in your life, teaches you how to be your best because of how they show up themselves.

Leadership is nothing short of a journey into one's soul.

As we work to engage with our truest selves, leadership, and life in general, requires a tremendous amount from us. It requires us to finish the report, drive the carpool, prepare for the earnings call, change directions, end the relationship, close the deal, and hold a hand. This journey into our souls is lifelong, takes us through varied landscapes, and invites us to place our feet on solid yet holy ground.

As a result, we shift our perspective on leaders. The word "leader" evokes images of authoritative generals, powerful executives, savvy politicians, and world-class athletes. While some of those people may very well be Connected Leaders, many people who hold those titles are not. Leadership is not about title, net worth, position, or power. Leaders are anyone—a child, a teenager, an adult—who inspires others to fearlessly soar and be their very best, not by being charismatic on stage, but by living an inspirational life as they:

- Create an emotionally safe environment in which others can share thoughts and feelings without being shamed, blamed, or tuned out.
- Are accountable themselves and invite others to accept responsibility for delivering on commitments, learning from mistakes, and performing at the highest level possible.
- Understand that leadership is an "and," not an "either/or." It means caring for people *and* doing what is tough to ensure that professional ethical, and behavioral standards are adhered to.
- Allow others to take a risk, fall down, and realize mistakes are potential wisdom in disguise.
- Share their stories and show up real, remembering that people do not trust perfection.
- Exhibit self-discovery and encourage others to do the same.

This kind of leadership requires everything we've got, and then some, because the path we walk as Connected Leaders will zigzag and be filled with unexpected obstacles. We will be led to, and will lead others to, summits with breathtaking views. Of course, this will only happen if we persevere with grit, be steadfast during what St. John of the Cross called "the dark night of the soul," and flourish because of lessons learned. Leadership is truly a light that flows from our struggles.

What I know for sure is those who commit themselves to being this type of Connected Leader live from a place of abundance, not scarcity; they believe humans are more delightful when we are real and there is plenty to go around. They enjoy strong results, whether it be enhanced shareholder value, more engaged teams, harmonious relationships at home, or an abiding sense of calm regardless of what storms rage around them.

Being a Connected Leader transforms loved ones into soul mates, families into havens, groups into cohesive teams, and workplaces into gateways that usher us and those we serve into possibility.

We Journey Together

While a student at Princeton Theological Seminary, I learned my calling was to listen to people's stories—to what was said and what was not said. I had begun cultivating this years earlier, as a member of a family whose dynamics could sometimes rival a Greek drama. Seminary just brought this gift more into the light. I was comfortable working in the shadows to help people learn about themselves. Actually, I was so fascinated by people's stories and my own, I went on to get yet another master's degree—this one in clinical social work so I could be a psychotherapist. This degree was not only a symptom of my obsessive need to prove my worthiness; it was also a genuinely good thing, since seminary had quickly taught me my calling had nothing to do with preaching, hermeneutics, and working on Sundays.

I have built on my calling as an executive coach and leadership consultant who was first trained as a therapist with a spiritual leaning. I am privileged to work with companies that are household names. I am honored to be a confidante to those who sit in corner offices and those who aspire to do so. I am invited by talented entrepreneurs to guide them and their organizations to a new level of success. I work with teams around the globe that want to do the hard work of fortifying trust and connection to enhance the success of their business.

I have the best job in the world. I listen to other people's stories so, as leaders, they can step into their true selves; and in doing so, I also get to dive into my stories. My work allows me to develop and tweak a philosophy that has significantly enhanced the wellbeing of many, while giving me a construct for my own journey.

In this work, I leverage three sacred items that grow our sense of Connected Leadership. The first is the power of stories—*liturgy*—which brings us together and helps us understand that we do not go through our experiences in isolation; we are connected through the similarities we discover as we tell our stories which could be the very thing, when shared, that helps someone else have hope and find their way. Second is the power of the table—*communion*—which reminds us that gathering together matters and sustains us; the table and stories nourish every single part of who we are. And third is the power of forgiveness—*redemption*—which sets the tone for how we approach ourselves and others after disruptive disappointments and horrific hurts, fully understanding that forgiveness is living with grace and gratitude while also honoring the importance of respectful boundaries.

Life and leadership have a way of knocking the ever-livin' snot out of us while also caressing us with moments of wonder and contentment. The struggle between our competent and flawed selves will always be something to be held in tension, lightly and gently. I am a wife and mother, sister and aunt, friend and colleague, who, despite professional competence, can be overwhelmed by my mistakes and the incongruity between how I *want* to show up and how I sometimes *actually* show up.

My desire to be empathetic is sometimes juxtaposed with unavailability, crabbiness, fear, or general overwhelm. I have to keep my self-righteous streak in check when I feel unappreciated and think fire and brimstone seems like an interesting option. As an Enneagram Two, I am damn good at building a loving haven and community, and yet, sometimes it would be best if I just stayed far out of sight when I am feeling taken advantage of. I am learning to stop myself from rushing to rescue others as a way to deal with my anxiety; I would have even tried to pull Jesus off the cross. I recognize my judgments, disdain, and even contempt can be activated when I am attacked or gaslit. Sometimes the fear of disconnection washes over me, and I envision driving off the road—because Lord have mercy—how much more can I take, and yet, I keep driving because God must think I am a world-class badass, and He must know. And, on some days, I catch the wind just right and sail through the storm.

We are complex human beings navigating a world of hurt and mess, joy and triumph. Connected Leaders find wisdom in the struggle, messiness, and daily rhythms.

As I bring dirty clothes into the laundry room, I see the painting our son, Matthew, created as a seven-year-old during the summer he mustered the courage to jump off the high dive. The painting, filled with bright primary colors, is of a diving board and a pool; it helps me to be mindful of what it takes to show up, walk to the edge, and let go. Doing this is not for the fainthearted but for those who choose courage over the known, honesty over pretense.

Matthew's painting reminds me that we both understand that the high dive was nothing compared to what it sometimes took to just move through our lives, one day at a time, staying connected to each other, during some really traumatic times thanks to the impact that divorce, illness, addiction, and abuse had on us. This painting is my daily inspiration to share my fears, embrace my vulnerabilities, and let people into the confusion I can feel. It is my call to write this book and begin to tell the story even when my inner critic says, "What could you possibly have to say?"

Today is a perfect day for the high dive, to trust I have something to say, and to move beyond fear to live and lead with connection. It is a perfect day for us to celebrate all we have in common, for this is a "we" journey, not a DIY life.

Let's get started. The world needs us to do so.

Chapter One

Wired to Connect: How Our Need to Connect Enhances Life and Leadership

---

"What kills a soul? Exhaustion, secret keeping, image management. And what brings a soul back from the dead? Honesty, connection, grace."
—Shauna Niequist

Lessons from a Bakery

Bob sits around boardroom tables negotiating deals with many, many zeros attached to them. He works in the world of hotel real estate and is often dealing with financial complexities that would make most of us cry uncle.

As a teenager, he sat around a different kind of table in Brooklyn, learning more than just how to fill cannolis and make cookie trays in the bakery owned by the parents of his then-girlfriend, now-wife. He learned how energizing it is to connect with people, telling stories that reveal who they are. His own parents were hardworking Depression era sculpted New Yorkers who created a strong community of connection; they were active in the school system, went to church down the

1

street from where they lived, participated in the rituals that marked the passing of days, and celebrated the mileposts of life with religious sacraments. They gathered on their stoop in the evening to socialize and were deeply rooted in their salt-of-the-earth values. They showed compassion by bringing food to their neighbors going through a tough time. They coparented with other adults, creating a strong network of eyes and ears from which the children could not escape. They sought support from friends and invested in the enriching rhythms of talking to people every day.

Decades later, during a leadership team meeting designed to build trust, Bob linked the experience of the bakery table to the leader he was becoming. He talked at length, surprising himself, about how working in that bakery provided him with a tremendous sense of security, safety, connection, and wellbeing despite the sadness, struggle, and fear one finds in any community. As he spoke, you could see the power of his experience fill him. In that moment, he came to see clearly what the neighborhood taught him and what the bakery table symbolized. His epiphany about when his leadership training really started both strengthened and humbled him.

That sense of deep belonging, experienced in a room smelling of butter and flour, and in a neighborhood of voices calling and families connecting, formed the foundation for his life at work and home. For Bob, the deal, regardless of how much it is financially worth, is all about the people. He can put himself in the shoes of those who sit across the table from him. He feels most alive sitting at a table enjoying his team's company, whether they are debriefing a business opportunity, strategizing at a team offsite, or sharing a meal. His team feels it too. The seductive, siren-like calls they often hear, as other potential employers court them, do not pull them away from Bob. They are loyal, successful, positively energized, and engaged, even during a global pandemic.

What is this recipe Bob learned in that bakery and applied throughout his life? How did he go from being an ordinary kid from Brooklyn to a beloved leader and talented executive? How did he evolve into a family man who knows his family's strong roots depend on shared experiences?

It's people like Bob who inspired me to write this book. He and many others remind me that while we are all searching for the Holy Grail, we come home when we discover that true connection starts within us and give ourselves permission to do the work to find it. I know firsthand what it is like to go from self-righteousness to humility. It is a realization that set me on the path to surrender and finally understand how the power of connection lives at the intersection of our professional and personal lives.

We Are Wired to Connect

We have a biological need to connect. It is wired into our brains and is as basic as our need for safety, food, and water. Acknowledging this need leads us to understand that our workplaces, educational and religious institutions, neighborhoods, and families are only going to thrive when we create ways to nourish our desire for connection: a biological need to be in community so we are safe, protected, purposeful, and thriving.

Much research is being done on how we are wired for connection. One example is the work of Matthew Lieberman, a professor in the departments of psychology, psychiatry, and biobehavioral sciences at the University of California, Los Angeles. Author of *Social: Why Our Brains Are Wired to Connect*, he writes, "The best bosses have to foster better connections between themselves and their team, among team members, and between team and other outside groups and individuals critical to success."[3] He goes on to discuss how this will create better communication, harmony that allows people to best serve the larger purpose, and a stronger attachment to the group.

Yet here is the thing; many people do not know how to deepen their connection to themselves, to a higher purpose, or to others *in healthy, sustainable ways.* And those who do know still struggle. The path of a Connected Leader outlines the way forward.

Enhancing the seven strategies that fuel connection is the work of a lifetime. We will not always manifest them. Mostly, we aspire to them. Sometimes we will hit the nail on the head, and sometimes we will miss the mark completely.

The required investment to walk this path of connection is high, yet the return is rich. Here's what we will need to strengthen the three types of connection to self, spirituality/purpose, and others:

- **Courage** is the still, small voice inside us that pushes us to be brave and authentic. It helps us to stay attuned to our feelings, take risks, and create boundaries that are put in place lovingly and respectfully to honor our own wellbeing. Courage pushes us outside of our comfort zone at the same time we want to curl up, eat a quart of rocky road, and live inside old patterns—even if they wreak havoc. Courage demands that we acknowledge our part and change what we can change.
- **Mindfulness** is about living life fully awake. Being mindful sharpens our experience while expanding our gratitude. When partnered up with grace, it helps us to experience the God of our understanding. It brings our attention to the moment even as the world urges us to text while having dinner with family, post on social media instead of being where our feet are, and take conference calls at our child's school play. Mindfulness is about being present, not flawless.
- **Vulnerability** is the willingness to say, "I have hurt others. I have damaged myself. I have made mistakes And I have doubts." In this way, we own our mess. When is showing vulnerability most powerful? When things do not fall exactly into place and trusted people are there to help us through. When we struggle with personal pain while healthy people serve as our witness. When we talk to an audience about our mistakes instead of our triumphs. When we wonder if we can deliver

the quarterly results or repair a relationship. Those who are vulnerable leave nothing on the field and turn toward the tribe instead of hanging out on the sidelines blaming others, hiding behind intellect, political views, education, or out-and-out-lies. Vulnerability means we are emotionally honest (in appropriate, purposeful ways) with those on whom we are willing to take a risk or already trust.

- **Resiliency** comes when we find the courage to embrace the pain, learn, get up, and try again. Living a connected life does not mean everything goes according to plan. Ironically, it often involves being brought to our knees. Who wants that? At times, I would rather be reading a Pottery Barn catalog and eating a danish. But living a connected life does not come by playing it safe. We flourish, we don't just bounce back, when we are willing to dig deep, rise up, and awaken.

- **Silence** gives us the insight, acceptance, and compassion to create our best lives. Imagine what would happen if more people practiced silence every day and had a routine of mindful solitude. If we let our friends, family, and colleagues speak instead of jumping in as soon as they take a breath. If we carved out time every day to quiet our minds, hear our thoughts, and tune into the wisdom that resides within. By going still, we improve our self-awareness, tap into the divine presence, and enhance connection to others. We awaken and learn to be open to the moment.

One day, an acquaintance told me about an argument she had had with her teenage daughter. It sounded like a familiar tale, something I could have easily been embroiled in with my own child. She ended her story with an exclamation points of sorts as she concluded with this, "I am right. I am always right." I thought she was kidding. She wasn't.

Truth be told, I could relate. We have all been there—choosing the safety of self-righteousness as opposed to the risky yet rewarding deep-dive of being vulnerable. Being right was more important to her

KAREN JOY HARDWICK, M.DIV., MSW

than learning what she could have done differently, accepting that feelings got churned up for her, and emotionally connecting to her child.

Fast-forward about five years. My acquaintance's daughter is struggling with anxiety and depression, despite keeping up a persona as the "golden girl." Word on the street is she self-medicates and encourages her peers to manage their anxiety with drugs and alcohol.

It is difficult to know what goes on behind closed doors, but this is what I know for sure: people struggle to connect with others who need to be perfect and are unwilling to talk about their own mistakes, like the girl's mother in this example. This young golden girl, struggling mightily, will hopefully take ownership of her choices and find a way to heal; no one else is to blame for what we each choose. Yet trauma and emotionally unsafe environments can exacerbate a temptation to choose a thing that bites us in the butt. Truth be told, the girl's mother is also most likely suffering, disconnected from herself and others, even though she might be unaware of this. Here is the thing: how we connect to or disconnect from ourselves can determine how much our family members (and our team members) share with us when they need a guiding hand or when they are doing battle. And they all do battle. So do we.

Our mistakes are most certainly carried by our children. I thought I would be the exception to that rule, but I wasn't. I am not unique or special. I did damage as a mother, and being a mother made me just a tinge crazier and more tightly wound. Why didn't anyone tell me how motherhood would increase my vulnerability to DEFCON levels? But here is the redeeming part: my willingness to take responsibility for the mistakes I made, make amends, and do differently impacts my son's emotional health and deepens our connection to one another.

I was a great mom before I had my son; I just knew I knew what was needed to be a good parent. I was clueless, arrogant, and wrinkle-free. Nineteen years in, I know differently. Motherhood has simply and totally brought me to my knees, so onward we go. There are times I nail it and others…well, let me just say Lord have mercy. I want my shining moments as one hell-of-an-awesome-mom to outshine my full-out-nutty-moments. But I am afraid they won't, and that the next generation will pay for my wounds I could not heal fast enough.

One way I connect more deeply to myself—as a mother, leader, and human being—is to gather feedback from those around me who I trust and who are also on an emotional, spiritual path. Another way is through tools like the Enneagram an assessment that helps shed light on our motivations, defense-survival tactics, and gorgeous potential.

I have learned, as a through and through Enneagram Two, that I am fueled by terror: terror that by articulating my needs, I will be rejected and humiliated (I am not delusional; this has happened in some chapters of my life, so it is a thing!). My defense against having my needs historically minimized or mocked was to focus on helping others. I became an Olympic-medal-winning helper: expending herculean efforts to help others feel loved, accepted, and cozy.

Now after grounding myself in sanity, I am still adept at creating emotionally safe havens for people that welcome them so they want to stay forever in my home, talk to me, soak up the loving energy, and eat the food I cook. Doing this fuels me; I simply love it. However, giving generously, in a healthy way, is in direct proportion to my willingness to care for myself as much as I care for others: to spend time filling my cup with as many joy-producing things as I am able, including solitude. And to soak up the love that surrounds me.

When terror moves into the driver's seat, however, I feel overlooked, unappreciated, and am fully in my Martha-mode (overworked, resentful, and not just a little pissy). It is best for me to keep my mouth shut during these times so I don't set off an emotional atomic bomb, guilting everyone for taking such advantage of good ol', wonderful, selfless me. I can out-Martha Martha.

I am learning (finally) to turn all the loving, yummy stuff also on myself. Honestly, it makes everything consistently smoother. When I connect to myself deeply and throw myself into the self-discovery process, I am, as my friend Ian Morgan Cron says in his book The Road Back to You: An Enneagram Journey to Self-Discovery, doing the healing work of a Two: "to work on their soul in solitude."[4]

My son Matthew, who is now nineteen, was walking out the door the other day and said over his shoulder, "Thanks, Mom. I am proud of all the work you are doing on yourself. It matters." (Translation: Thanks, Mom, for no longer getting in my lane all the time with your incessant lecturing, "helping" (a.k.a. controlling), and trying so hard to make me happy.)

As leaders in the workplace and not just the family room are we owning our stories? Are we working on being our true, best selves? And are we creating psychologically safe places for those entrusted to our care, including ourselves?

And if the neurologically based need called connection is so important, then why are we suffering from the symptoms of disconnection? If our pull to connect is tidal in its strength, then why are so many of us suffering so much of the time?

The Conundrum of Connection

We crave connection, yet we often turn from the kind that can truly heal.

We are often in a crisis of disconnection. Many of our teens are struggling way beyond the "normal" adolescent angst. Families can be isolated, marriages are often lackluster, many leaders are misbehaving, and too many communities are unsafe as unspeakable violence increases. People are divisive, hurting, and rageful. Social media is often used as a platform to lash out with anger and judgment. Many of us, including very young children, are glued to screens and foregoing face-to-face conversations.

Our workplaces are filled with people whose disengagement contributes to low morale and decreased productivity. Uncertainty and worldwide fear leave us searching for enemies to blame. And, all of these emotional, spiritual, and behavioral symptoms are occurring within a context of "more": more information, screens, frenzied activity...more of absolutely everything except the kind of connection that creates understanding and healing.

At this crossroads, we each need to make a conscious choice: Do we want to take the "road less traveled" and risk the known for deeper connections? Can we breathe in courage and dive beneath the water line into ourselves so we can be a shining light for others? Can we encourage the kinds of conversation that allow for compassion to emerge as the most powerful voice in our communities? Or do we want to remain "right," using our shame to bully others, our rigidity to feel superior, and our woundedness to gaslight?

If what we want is to build the new, instead of to rage against the old, then we have to dig deep within ourselves.

Understanding Connection to Deepen It

Through decades of work and observation, I have coined a definition of connection:

> *Connection is the deep abiding sense that three things co-exist to create emotional wholeness, relational wellbeing, and spiritual strength: we learn about ourselves through reflection, self-discovery, and honest self-exploration; we develop a sense of purpose through spiritual practices that invite us to be in relationship with something bigger than ourselves; we develop ties to others through shared experiences that allow us to feel safe, heard, and accepted, and that deepen our mutual sense of wellbeing.*

In families, healthy connections allow children to:

- Feel understood so they develop the internal strength necessary to navigate their own life, tough parts and all.
- Advocate for themselves and make self-affirming decisions.

- Trust they can survive, own, regulate, and process emotions in constructive ways.
- Be the experts of their own lives by discovering who they truly are.
- Navigate frustration, sadness, and failure.
- Know firsthand the power found in rising up and flourishing after a mistake.
- Witness adults being committed to their own wellbeing.
- Seek out emotionally healthy, safe people with whom to have relationships.

This also means parents step back from fixing, assuaging, rescuing, and marketing our children. Through the power of connection, children are more strongly positioned to build a productive, resilient, and healthy life for themselves, including choosing friends who walk the same path. Through the power of connection, children are gifts entrusted to us instead of projects to be managed.

Connection encourages adults to turn toward others and integrate a deeper sense of intimacy by:

- Understanding their own emotional needs while being open-hearted toward others.
- Healing their wounds and owning their stories, chapter by chapter.
- Owning their emotional, spiritual, mental, and physical well-being.
- Disagreeing in ways that are constructive and respectful.
- Balancing the "we" while taking care of the "I".
- Taking risks to live courageously and model vulnerability.
- Setting healthy boundaries rooted in self-care *and* compassion for the other.
- Knowing their own purpose and integrating that into a larger community.

And in the workplace, connection contributes mightily to a company's success and competitive advantage as it:

- Enhances personal wellbeing, which contributes to positive business metrics like engagement.
- Strengthens a person's gifts and allows them to explore what is tripping them up.
- Provides a psychologically safe environment which encourages trust, innovation, risk-taking, curiosity, and self-awareness.
- Improves the quality of decisions, communication, and collaboration.
- Awakens appreciation for each other's contributions.
- Focuses on creating cultures founded on abundance and not scarcity, collaboration and not comparison.

Connection is not a one-and-done. Even the healthiest families, individuals, and workplaces cannot and will not connect perfectly and consistently. We are human: complex beings that can retreat into anger and blame, resistance and denial. When healthy connections are valued, however, we come out of our defensive postures to share, reach out, make amends, and begin again.

The Power of Discernment

At times, it is not always wise to connect, and those times are important to note.

It might have to do with emotional stuff and relational patterns you have going on. It might have to do with the other person's emotional and relational patterns. Regardless, it is important to hit the pause button, realize that "no" is a holy word, and dig deeper into yourself. This is the time to explore any unfinished emotional business you might have, recognize the courage it takes to walk away from people who are not good for your wellbeing, and be careful not to confuse manipulative, charming behavior with the actual change it takes to heal a relationship. Unless people are involved in a transformative structure, they will continue to be the same, even if their superficial behaviors are designed to have you think differently; some of these structures include having a gifted and compassionate therapist, working the twelve steps with a spiritually fit sponsor, and participating in other deep, healing work like spiritual direction or a coaching process with a clinically-trained coach.

It is important to create space from certain people who repeatedly behave in ways that are damaging. I cannot say this enough; believe people when they continually show you who they are. Do not fall in love with how you can fix them. We have the emotional and spiritual right to protect ourselves from people whose consistent emotional, mental, and relational behaviors and patterns are toxic to us at work and in life.

My general rule of thumb is that if the behavioral and relational pattern has continued despite your efforts to address dynamics directly and to give the person time to change, it might be wiser to wish the person well and adieu. There comes a time when we realize not everyone is meant to be a part of our intimate circle or ongoing journey. This process is not easy; it is complicated and complex. It involves working through resentments, sometimes trauma, often emotional pain, and moving toward true forgiveness, which does not mean you have to have someone over for tea. It is best to work through this with trusted advisors who can help us create boundaries in self-respecting ways, ensure our side of the street is clean, and move toward the forgiveness that frees us.

Moving on in this way is courageous and self-compassionate work. It is significantly different from an emotional cut-off, ghosting, or the silent treatment. People are sent our way to teach us valuable lessons about how to honor ourselves, say no to things we once accepted but are just not okay with anymore, and step into our precious worthiness. Our most powerful teachers are often those who have created pain in our lives, often times unbeknownst to them because they are emotionally asleep and acting out of their own repetitive trances.

I have been doing this inner work on myself for a long time, and just a few weeks ago, I had a huge epiphany which startled me. The truth is I had been dimming my light, backing away from a higher level of influence in my career, and choosing not to fully step into my gifts. I had wondered, for a while, what was fueling this pattern of mine. One morning, during my Centering Prayer, it came to me, as clearly as possible, that a major contributing factor to this pattern in my life was how the silent treatment has been used in my family.

Make no mistake, the silent treatment is emotional abuse. It is random, punishing, and undermining. The one who is being attacked by silence never knows when it is coming next or what triggered it. The one who dishes it out spends tremendous psychic energy validating their silence.

Through a variety of silent-treatment tactics I have witnessed first-hand, I learned that not staying focused on making others feel good would bring on the wrath of withering silence. To avoid the punitive, stony silences that could last days, weeks, or years, I did everything I could to mind-read, be thoughtful, and please the easily triggered ones. Except there is a small, teeny-tiny problem: they were never going to be pleased and I was bound to make a misstep. That is part of the seductive, toxic hook: they who will never be pleased do everything they can to make those around them hustle to please them.

My father was an expert in the silent treatment. He would freeze my mother out for days: never letting her know why he was angry or jealous or whatever the hell it was and feeling a sick sense of power and justification as he found ways to blame her for things that were not hers to own. It would destroy her (as if she needed any more stress). He would turn the same rejecting silence on me—usually triggered by his jealousy of my relationship with my mother or my childhood triumphs at school, such as they were.

And because we lived at times in crazy-town, my mother would also freeze her sister out, which was heartbreaking since my mom knew firsthand how poisonous the silent treatment was. As much as I adored my mom, the way she treated my aunt upset me; I could never really understand why my mom was so mad about things I thought, even as a child, did not seem fair to my aunt. I knew my mom was activated by her own jealousies and fears, looking for things she could pin on my aunt instead of dealing with the pain inside of herself. My aunt wound up apologizing for things she never did wrong to please my mom who would never be pleased.

The lesson I learned was to be cautious of shining, success, and enjoying your life. When people shone, the weapon of silence could and would be wielded. When my aunt enjoyed her life, my mother rejected her. When my aunt did not show up in ways my mom expected, silence would be weaponized. When I was close to my mother, my father would sulk into a stony silence that would last for long periods of time. And if you committed the heinous crime of not being perfectly focused on making others feel special, freezing-cold silences would be dished up for days, weeks, or years. As I moved into my adult life, similar patterns continued.

As I asked this question one recent morning—*why don't I allow myself to fully embrace a bigger professional platform and step onto the stage*—it was like a veil lifted immediately. This is how self-discovery works: layer by layer we go deeper over time, connecting to our inner intuition as we have the capacity to do. The more open and willing we are to understand, the more is revealed.

In that moment I remembered a wise person once said, "You come so close to professional greatness, and then you back away. Why?" Her words haunted me for over fifteen years; she was right. I chalked up putting my career on the back burner to my choice to put family first. Yet, as I unpacked this statement on the morning I had this epiphany, it dawned on me: I also, and very importantly, stepped away from having a more influential, public voice because of the abusive silences I endured and witnessed for years. These silences trained me to believe that when I was happy or successful or anything less than perfectly focused on making certain people feel like they were a top priority, I risked rejection and being cut out.

It is painful and traumatic enough to experience hurtful behavior; it is another thing entirely to experience a push-pull pattern over many a season. The repetition of it further exacerbates our hurt. The longer the pattern goes on, the more we try to twist ourselves into a pretzel to please those who will not be pleased and the more we do damage to ourselves.

Our own complicity is the big take away, period. It is not about blaming or holding people hostage with resentments. Because relationships can create a tremendous sense of wellbeing or can cause damage, our job is to discern what we need to learn from each relationship to live our best life by tuning in to what lifts us up and what tears us down.

I realized I was the one who had to change, be courageous, and stop fearing that I would be rejected. Instead, I renewed my focus on creating goodness for myself with the God-given gifts entrusted to me.

We are all finding our way. We are all susceptible to adopting unhealthy patterns of behavior when we are triggered. Those who put in the hard work of self-connection get more adept at recognizing their own unhealthy patterns and take responsibility for their behavior more quickly and completely. They also understand when there is real emotional danger and when to have clear boundaries. More on that later.

At this point in my journey, I would say the goal is to learn as much as we can from everyone and every experience, with an open heart, a curious mind, and a trust in the spiritual process. To use every situation to elevate our growth, wellbeing, and ability to shine the love of God through all we do. To break the destructive cycles we participate in and might pass on to others like a baton. To realize that when we live life from a connected, contemplative, conscious perspective, everything belongs as a part of our learning.

We might not always get the apology we want and often deserve. The other parties involved might not see the situation the same way: their denial might be too strong, and their emotional journey might require a different process. If we have checked our thinking with trusted, healthy others, and it is clear we have nothing to make amends for, then our side of the street is clean.

It is not about the other person. It is only about what we are learning, and that is between God and us. Therefore, it is essential that we let the other person go with compassion, wishing them well, and being clear that no longer participating in a destructive dynamic is what serves our leadership at work and in life.

Doubling Down on Self-Knowledge

Here's the thing. We all get triggered and can lash out with a primitive viciousness; I have been known to make Medusa seem like Miss Congeniality. Whether we are CEO or graduate student, priest or choirboy, we craft defenses early on in our lives to protect ourselves. And thank goodness for these! It is because of these defenses that we survive all kinds of nuttiness. However, these defenses can eventually become our default setting in unhealthy ways and create havoc in our lives.

As we do this work, we learn to be compassionate toward others and accept it is not our job to change the crazy in them. It is hard enough to address the crazy found in ourselves, but we must, one day at a time. When Matthew was eight, he said to me, "Mom, your crazy is showing." Shocking how he knew it and I didn't. As it says in the Old Testament, and I am paraphrasing, "A child will lead them." If we are awake to what our kids are teaching us, we know this is indubitably true.

While there are many ways to do this life-affirming yet downright difficult work of self-discovery and healing, I strongly believe in the power of therapy with a well-trained therapist who is also working on their own wounds. Working with a coach who has clinical training can also be powerful and transformative. Top leaders in organizations who invest in their people by providing them with a clinically-trained leadership coach are giving a priceless gift.

Additionally, the twelve steps are a way of life. I know firsthand how they invite us into a life of rigorous self-honesty; connection is the opposite of addiction, and the power of a healthy recovery community is worth every step. We are all recovering from something, and since we live in a culture in which addiction seems to be winning at times, the twelve steps, when done lovingly and intentionally, contribute to a healthy spiritual and emotional life. It works if you work it.

Another powerful tool is the Enneagram, an assessment which has nine basic personality types. I have taken and used many assessments in my lifetime; the Enneagram is hands-down my favorite because of its amazingly rich content from an emotional, spiritual, and relational perspective: helpful in professional and personal settings. It teaches us that we adopt certain ways of being during childhood to help us feel safe. As we mature, these patterns influence how we look at the world, motivate our behavioral patterns, and sometimes get stuck in ways of relating that are not in our best interest.

I use the Enneagram with my leadership clients; it is transformative. I refer to my own assessment report daily; one copy of my report sits on my nightstand and another one sits on my desk. It has deepened my recovery, self-knowledge, and willingness to grow. It has also taken off what was left of my blinders (actually, ripped off) and brought me to my knees while waking me up. Not all Enneagram assessments are created equal, so I strongly suggest using one that is reliable and valid while yielding a report that is chock-full of eureka-level insights.[5]

The whole purpose of connecting consciously with ourselves is to free us from patterns that limit our joy and push us into making decisions that don't necessarily work out well. When we don't own our struggles or understand our unconscious motivations, we can participate in all kinds of insanities. On the other hand, when we are too eager to please and own things not ours to own, our emotional and spiritual abilities are stunted. Learning to recognize what we truly own emotionally and relationally, and what others want us to falsely own, is critical to our wellbeing.

A client of mine called upset the other day. A colleague of his had been quite erratic and disruptive for years: temper tantrums, lies, manipulative tactics. His behavior was exceedingly difficult on those around him. He was not self-aware and could not see the impact his behavior had on others; in his mind he was always right and justified. He did not own his stuff; he tried to convince those around him that they were responsible for his behavior. Unfortunately, his sales performance was outstanding, and so the organization kept him, which was crazy-making for his peers and team. My client was the Chief Marketing Officer, and although he had limited interactions with this dude, he still had to preserve a professional relationship.

My client decided he was done trying to have meaningful conversations with the sales guy: conversations in which he would try and help the sales guru see how his behavior hurt others. The conversations landed on deaf ears, resulted in denial and blame, and nothing changed. So, my client made a healthy decision to create a reasonable boundary, limit his interactions, and stop efforts to be emotionally open; although he would continue to be professionally communicative. As it turned out, the sales colleague became furious when my client chose not to have a social lunch with him. He wrote a scathing email blaming the Chief Marketing Officer for being unavailable and selfish. He went into detail about all that he was doing to be a world-class colleague (note: this was delusional) and how the refusal to go out for a social lunch was a grave injustice.

If nothing else, the Chief Marketing Officer breathed a sigh of relief; the rant of the email was proof positive that his decision to limit interactions was clearly the right decision. By not even responding to the email, he put the onus where it belonged: on the sales guy, who hopefully would one day wake up and accept his own behavior.

I want to invite as many people as possible to wake up to the freedom that can come from connecting consciously with ourselves, owning our stuff, and as a result, inspiring others to do the same. This matters a great deal in the workplace, at home, and in life, in general as we show up, grow up, and wake up with grace, acceptance, gratitude, and forgiveness.

Work and life would be easy if it were not for the people.

The Power of Boundaries In the Service of Connection

Knowing how to put loving guardrails and boundaries in place—which differ from withering, harsh silences—is an important part of the connection wisdom. Let's make the distinction clearly:

- *Boundaries* come from a place of grounded sanity, humility, vulnerability, and self-compassion: we recognize that it is not our job to fix, rescue, and save others but to provide them with the opportunity to grow up, wake up, and step up. Boundaries are empowerment-creators and connection-makers. Boundaries mean we have clear rules of engagement and adhere to them. We take care of ourselves when those rules are ignored and have clear consequences designed to invite others to be accountable for their behavior. When we honor our boundaries, we stop rushing in with a response or a solution or explanation. Boundaries occur when we get tired of responding to others in ways that were about assuaging our own anxiety or giving too much of our time, resources, emotions to prove how loveable we are. Boundaries occur when we take our hands off the steering wheel and give those we love and lead the dignity of finding their way and owning their actions. Boundaries need no explanation or defense: we don't have to take out a billboard announcing a boundary, we just change our behavior.
- *Withering, harsh silences* are designed to punish; they come from a place of insanity, ego, shame, and self-loathing. They are usually a response to a story the silent-treatment-dispenser has going on in their own head. They are executed in a way so to blame someone for something not theirs to own. They are

abusive and destructive. They usually come out of nowhere, are randomly dished out to throw people off, and create an unsafe, relational dynamic. They are designed to be a power-grab and are manipulative and passive-aggressive. They have a toxic quality to them because they are created to destroy and shame. They give the one who is dishing out the silent treatment a twisted sense of power. Those who are attacked by these silences never know when they are going to happen but know they will happen again.

Paying attention to the emotional and spiritual energy of others is important as we consider the power of connection. There are times other people are just not ready for connection. This is not meant to pigeonhole people, criticize, or categorize them. They are on a different path and timetable.

So, take it from me, a recovering Higher Power. No one wants to be saved. No one wants to be fixed. No one wants to entertain how their behavior has been damaging to you unless they truly are ready to own their dynamic. Once you have had a conversation or two with someone at work or home about their behavior that is damaging to the connection, and there is no change, it is time to consider boundaries.

So be mindful of when it is safe to connect and when it is best to take your space, create a boundary, and focus on your own wellbeing at work and at home. Consider these examples:

- When someone is actively involved in addictions they will not be emotionally available. Translation: do not try to rescue, lecture, plead, or engage.
- It isn't only people who suffer from addictions who may not be engaged and interested in connection; it can also be difficult to have a healthy relationship with people struggling with untreated mental illnesses, or people who are emotionally unavailable or are simply not working on their spiritual and relational recovery.

- It is also not safe to connect with people who are in any kind of emotionally regressed state, actively raging, or verbally/physically violent. They are so blinded that all they can see is how you are their scapegoat, punching bag, and fuel tank. All the empathy, insight, and wisdom you possess will not save them. They have to find their own wisdom and recovery; and until they do, they will not think twice about trying to destroy anyone who gets in the way of their disease and crazy thinking. This is how it works, regardless of how big your superhero cape is.
- If someone's basic MO is any of the above dynamics or consistently blames, scapegoats, and pushes someone back on their heels, it is not safe to connect. Turn to others for support instead. If this happens at work, ask for help in working through this. If it occurs at home, find someone who can help you see the situation for what it is and help you decide how to best keep yourself safe on all levels while dealing with a family member who is in the throes of this type of behavior.

Remember many of us find ourselves in a situation where a therapist, the twelve step community, a trusted advisor at work, or a spiritual director can help us find our way.

Here are my basic rules of thumb about connection in all parts of our personal and professional lives:

- If you don't feel safe, you aren't.
- If you tell yourself you can love and understand someone in a way they have never before experienced, run. You are not their savior. You are not that special or powerful. I promise you: you will not be the exception.
- Choose the time for a conversation carefully if you must connect with someone who is really struggling. Have reinforcements nearby.

- Not everyone was designed for us to intimately connect with, even though we can learn from everyone.
- Find your tribe: people who will be truth-tellers, who are also doing their self-discovery work, and who consistently help you to feel joyful, safe, heard, and understood when you are in their presence.

As important as connection is, being honest and realistic about ways to enhance healthy connections is critical as we lead ourselves and others.

Taking Our Cue from Nature

During a fall hike through a stand of aspens and then again snow-shoeing through the same stand months later, I wondered why I was so drawn to the aspens. After some quick research, I discovered why the aspens, beautiful and ethereal, call to me and why the wisdom I seek continues to be mirrored in nature.

Aspens survive and thrive through a connected root system, shared with their fellow aspens. They reproduce by sprouting shoots from their roots, which allow them to stay connected to the other aspens while being deeply rooted individually. They are so connected that they are a single living organism, able to withstand threats, share nutrients, and support one another. The life and health of one affects the whole.

We can be inspired by this idea of shared roots. To become human versions of aspens, it is not enough to be wired to connect. We must learn *how* to deeply connect and tap into that connection. The Connected Leader approach and its seven key attributes are inextricably woven, sharing the same roots and inviting us to deepen connection. The Connected Leader:

1. **Connects Consciously**
2. **Listens Deeply**
3. **Exhibits Empathy**

4. **Practices Curiosity**
5. **Demonstrates Accountability**
6. **Navigates Chaos Comfortably**
7. **Walks with Courage-based Confidence**

We will explore each of these in detail in the following chapters as both individual attributes and as a collective. Like the aspen tree, Connected Leaders are grounded in the need to share shoots from our roots and the belief that, only together, can we experience the true gifts of connection.

Chapter Two

Connects Consciously: Doing the Work

"To be nobody but yourself in a world which is doing its best, night and day, to make you everybody else—means to fight the hardest battle which any human being can fight; and never stop fighting."

—E.E. Cummings

The Power of Chasing Slow

Over the course of one week some years ago, my husband told me he felt hurt because I was not spending enough time with him, a CEO client told me he needed more frequent conversations with me, and even my yoga teacher felt I was not spending enough time on my practice! *Were they kidding?* I wanted to run away from it all, but I had nowhere to go.

Regardless of my efforts to take care of myself, do my work, and tend to my family, I felt like I was failing miserably (this is a recurring theme for me) and tumbling into sabotaging self-criticism.

Raised with the clear message that it was my job to put everything and everyone before myself, I grew up as the caretaker of my younger siblings and my terminally ill mother. I turned that skill, crafted through years of sacrifice, people-pleasing, and emotional angst, into an initial career as a therapist. Along the way, I made decisions that did not serve me well because I used the same litmus test for those decisions as I did growing up: were people feeling happy? Was I providing folks with what they wanted? Was I feeling powerful because people needed me?

The complaints I received from my husband, client, and yoga teacher, however, served as the impetus for one of the many turning points in my life as I committed to discovering how I could connect more consciously, with only twenty-four hours per day.

After I got this feedback that people were feeling disconnected from me, I started to get up early—real early—to watch the day break, get caffeinated in silence, and listen for the ancient wisdom within to guide me. I knew I did not have any more to give, and I was not sure I wanted to give it even if I had it.

This early-rising, stillness-seeking, coffee-drinking time allowed me to connect more consciously with myself: that was the game-changer. I had always been a fan of such practices, but this time it was different; I was doing it consistently—on a daily basis—not randomly, and *for me*, not to just check it off the list. What a difference this little shift has made. It's not that I have more time, even though the time I have feels more plentiful and intentional. I have more energy. Focus. Presence. As a result, those around me feel they have more time with me because *I* have more time with me.

I have come up with new strategies for my business during the quiet of the a.m., deepened my prayer life, and determined what I need to do to free myself from patterns that no longer serve me. I readjust my parenting. Read inspiring poems, the Bible, and meditations. I confront my struggles and darkness. I find myself and God in the morning quiet through a variety of mindful practices, including centering prayer. I hear the whispers that empower me to live boldly and go to where the joy is slow. When others ask how I live how I live and do what I do, I tell them about this practice. Changing just one thing ended up changing everything: how I do the morning is how I do the day.

I used the feedback I got from important people in my life as an opportunity to *chase slow.* To accomplish more and do less. To be more intentional, less distracted. To give to myself so I could give to others. Chasing slow does not mean I put my ambitions or dreams on hold, nor does it mean that I passively sit around waiting for someone to show up with bonbons. However, doing nothing is a self-loving strategy that allows us to rest and recharge.

A few years ago, as I was struggling with my parenting, a therapist I was working with said, "If nothing changes, if nothing changes." He taught me to be fearlessly honest with myself and about myself, and to be the change I needed. He helped me to break through my denial and do the hard work of seeing how I was part of the problem. I put his words on a sign that rests in our keeping room; I see those words, absorb them, apply them, and quietly thank Nick each day.

Being human is hard work. There are days filled with grief when we hear about or experience losses we cannot comprehend. There are days of boredom, tedious details, and struggle. Moments, not even necessarily triggered by emotional struggles, in which a deep sense of separateness aches in our bones, making us feel restless and depleted, apathetic and disconnected, lonely and untethered. Alone.

There are days where the tiny pinpricks of irritation cascade into an anger begging for release. Times where waves of discontent wash out wellbeing. Moments where there is not enough coffee ice cream in the world, because I am just downright tired, somewhat disbelieving, and skeptical that anything matters. Being human is hard and messy.

Then something shifts, the light begins to creep in, and we are reminded that grace oftentimes shows up in the bottom of the ninth. This is what it means to be a Connected Leader: understanding that life and leadership are not feel-good salutes to positivity but marathons of self-discovery and emotional honesty.

When I ran the New York Marathon, all 26.2 miserable miles, I passed many cute little cafés in the five boroughs. All I could picture was sitting down at one of those tables, saying, "Give me a double latte," and calling someone to rescue me from this ridiculous way to spend a perfectly good autumn day. Sometimes this is how I feel about life, too: can someone just come and pick me up? And then I realize that I am the one who must pick myself up by deciding how I spend my energy, chase slow so I have enough inner fuel, and honor time with myself along with having the right people around me.

It is how we run the race, how we fuel ourselves when we don't necessarily see the finish line, and how we remain deeply anchored in the things that matter even when we feel like we don't. There is not one among us—CEO, newly-minted MBA graduate, parent, recently transitioned executive—who does not need the healing balm of connection that starts with connecting consciously with ourselves, with chasing slow.

Consciously Connecting to Lead from Within

Today's business environment is complex—so is family life. We make our environments even more complex than they need to be because we forget our power is nourished by self-discovery and tending to the basics: sleeping, eating, exercising, connecting, and having a daily spiritual practice. We strengthen what we practice, and we become a walking billboard for those practices.

What used to be good enough for leaders just three decades or even five years ago no longer holds, and for good reason; intellectual, functional, and academic leadership is not enough. Leadership is a synergistic call to action that blends cognitive, emotional, spiritual, and intuitive gifts. Skill-based competencies are table stakes. What truly matters is the ability to empower and inspire others via connecting to our self. We can no longer MBA our way into the leadership that empowers, inspires, and transforms.

In a world that is increasingly competitive, leaders navigate globalization, the twenty-four-seven tsunami of information, regulatory requirements, and the search for talent. They also are wise to learn how to be curious, empathetic, self-aware, and mindful. Given these ongoing pressures, many leaders stumble by relying too heavily on old business models, which are often outdated and fueled by fear and scarcity. Staying stuck feels safe, but it is dangerous. The invitation is to move into connection and abundance—and yes, this takes some work to say the least.

In the same way, we who are leaders in places other than the corporate workplace must also step carefully around the many landmines: monitoring social media so it does not suck the life out of ourselves or our children; addressing complex social-political issues with clarity and compassion; dealing with incivility; balancing tolerance with standing for something; being aware of the bullying omnipresent on playgrounds, locker rooms, workplaces...and the ubiquitous push to be more, have more, do more.

This is a lot! It is all coming toward us so fast that we often don't make the time to pause, process, and consciously connect. As leaders in corporate worlds, families, and communities, we want to find a way to make sense of the pressure and find answers to the questions with which we, our employees, our children, and our friends struggle.

In order to lead themselves and others into the Connection Era, every part of a leader must be engaged so they can pull the right tool at the right time and discern which tool is needed. Is it an intellectual resource? Recalling the latest research trends? An emotional solution? A spiritual means? A relational intervention?

It is by chasing slow and going within that leaders develop the discernment necessary to know how to respond in each situation and what type of response is best suited. We all know that situations arise where analysis and cognitive solutions are not enough. Times occur when, regardless of empathy, interpersonal dynamics will not be resolved. Scenarios transpire where "gut" responses must be put on hold so analytics can be double-checked.

Connected Leaders learn how, when, and where to engage which pieces so they can think boldly and guide others. And they develop the ability to do this by discovering the wisdom that comes from going within and chasing slow, the weightlifting for the soul that sharpens our discernment so we can better respond to the multitude of people, potential, and problems that come across our path.

Leadership is an inside job.

First Things First

Consciously connecting means we connect with ourselves to awaken, connect with a Higher Source to understand our spiritual essence and purpose, and connect with others in healthier ways as a result of connecting more deeply to ourselves and our spiritual purpose.

And while connecting consciously often includes having some kind of meditative practice, it is more a way of living that includes a wide variety of practices designed to deepen self-discovery. It is the desire to learn more about one's self: motivations, strengths, unresolved emotional pain. As we discover our true selves, we typically deepen our relationship to the God of our understanding and hone a more finely tuned sense of our own purpose while we are here in human school.

Connecting consciously is a combination of practices that strengthen emotional wholeness, spiritual strength, and relational health. It is the mental-physical-psychological synergy that allows people to live and lead with the perseverance, gratitude, and grace that life and work requires in order for us to move through our days with an enhanced presence, courage, and graciousness.

We cannot be present to others and connect consciously with them if we are not connecting with ourselves. The Harvard Business Review Emotional Intelligence series said this in an essay written by Ramus Hougaard and Jacqueline Carter entitled *If You Aspire to be a Great Leader, Be Present*, "In a recent survey of more than one thousand leaders, those who show up with a more mindful presence manifest the optimal strategy to engage their people, create better connections, and improve performance."[6]

If we are not okay with our vast array of emotions, how can we listen to someone else's sadness, anxiety, or joy? If we have not accepted our own imperfections, how can we ever be someone that others feel comfortable around, both at home and at work?

No one does this perfectly. And yet we show up and begin anew every day.

Jay Wolverton, the former CEO and founder of one of the largest engineering firms in Georgia, now the chief growth officer for a large national firm and a leader in the industry, says he turns off all devices, music, and distractions as he drives so he can enjoy the silence, hear the power of his own voice, reflect, and pray.

Scott Murphy, an executive who has held senior level roles at organizations like Turner Broadcasting, Ogilvy, and The Boys and Girls Clubs of America talks about the calming effect his mountain house has on him as he intentionally unplugs.

My friend, Susan Packard, who cofounded HGTV and was their former Chief Operating Officer says this about the practices that promote a peace of mind, a mindfulness, and an enhanced emotional intelligence:

> *"A huge benefit of these practices in the workplace is that you don't show up spring-loaded; you learn how to take a breath before instinct takes over or defer to silence when cutting words are ripe for unloading. This is hard stuff, pressing pause when you might otherwise respond with heat, but it gets much easier the more you practice. Moreover, you become a better listener, and a more creative worker."[7]*

Susan should know—she rose to the highest ranks of leadership in a tough industry. She now facilitates retreats on mindfulness and Centering Prayer. Having attended some of her retreats I know how powerfully she shows up—fully human and eager to guide others through the inside-out practices of self-discovery so more leaders can balance success with grace, power with resilience.

The Latin root of "inspire" means to "breathe or blow into." It was originally used to indicate that a spiritual or divine being was imparting a truth. Therefore, Connected Leaders, who inspire others, are in touch with an unseen force that breathes wisdom and discernment into themselves and others.

Rainer Maria Rilke said it powerfully in *Letters to a Young Poet*, "But your solitude will be a support and a home for you, even in the midst of very unfamiliar circumstances, and from it you will find all your paths."[8]

Michael Gervais, sports psychologist and founder and facilitator of the podcast *Finding Mastery*, has a saying that is one of his hallmarks. He says, "Every day we have an opportunity to create a living masterpiece."[9]

Connected Leaders know their masterpiece begins by finding wisdom in the difficulties and connecting to the whole fabric of their life: a masterpiece created from the whole of their life, suffering and loss, joy and love.

The Path to Purpose

Connecting with yourself means forging a spiritual path regardless of how you experience a Higher Power. The most effective leaders I know have some type of spiritual practice, belief, and relationship. It is the very thing that helps them flourish in the face of daunting odds, restores them to sanity, and allows them to experience the interconnectedness of all things as they determine how to create a masterpiece of their life. It encourages them to accept all parts of their story, not denying the uglier chapters or exaggerating the pretty ones. It guides them to hit the pause button. It helps them to stop talking and tune into their intuition.

As we work on our spiritual practices and our spiritual practices then work on us, we begin to deepen our sense of our own purpose and wrestle with the big questions: Why are we here? Why do we do what we do? What can others teach me? There is never one conclusive answer to any of these questions as the more we seek answers, the more questions we have; yet the journey of a Connected Leader keeps us open to our purpose and intrigued by the evolving answers.

This sense of Purpose allows us to accept that we can learn from everyone and every occurrence. Living from our purpose does not mean spiritual bliss; it does mean we will come into contact with and discover our true self more frequently and intentionally.

By nourishing our connection with a spiritual experience and creating a deep sense of purpose, we become more available to connecting with others in ways that break us wide open and elevate our growth, whether it be discussing a potential acquisition with our attorneys, holding a friend's hand as they wrestle with a husband's illness, or guiding our child on how to trust his gut.

As we move to the next chapter to explore *listening deeply*, we will see how each of the attributes of being a Connected Leader play off of and contribute to the others. The Connected Leader model is not a collection of individual parts but a synergistic whole. They are all… well, connected.

Connection Reflection for Strategy One: Connects Consciously

o Find someone or a few trusted souls to walk this path with you: a therapist, a clinically trained coach, a twelve step group, or other guides that help you to connect consciously with yourself and strengthen your self-discovery.

o Begin to journal your thoughts, experiences, and feelings. Make a list of mistakes you have made, and practice letting yourself feel compassion and empathy; we do the best we can, and when we learn to do better, we do. Move toward doing better with self-compassion so you can extend this level of understanding, connection, and empathy to others.

o Develop a practice that allows you to connect to the larger purpose in life, a spiritual sense of connectedness.

o Come to your work every day with an intentionality to slow down, hit the pause button, and be mindfully present to the work and people. One conversation at a time. One email at a time. One meeting at a time.

Chapter Three

Listens Deeply: The Sound of Silence

"The soul always knows what it needs to heal itself.
The challenge is to silence the mind."
—Caroline Myss

Lessons from an Early Riser

Over lunch one day, Steve shared his frustration with me as we met to discuss his leadership goals for the year. As a CFO of a publicly traded company, he was increasingly annoyed because he felt as if his day did not belong to him. He enjoyed his job and with whom he worked, but he was feeling burned out; and while he was a religious man, he was not in touch with a more peaceful way to live and work. He felt distracted in all facets of his life. His family saw him as the cranky, disengaged guy who dashed out in the morning and returned in the evening, cell phone glued to his ear. Despite having the title he had coveted for years and the financial security for which he had worked so hard, he felt like he was on a slippery slope.

As the conversation came to a lull, I asked him, "Could you get up earlier before anyone else in your house?"

"Sure," he replied. "But why?"

I explained that I value rising early, long before the rest of my family awakens. I gather my thoughts as the coffee kicks in. I set my intentions for the day. I talked about how the idea was not to fill the quiet but to just exist with it. I shared that until I had committed to such a ritual, I, too, felt like I was running to catch up all day long while falling increasingly behind, feeling grouchy and rushed, and finding ways to blame those around me.

I ended by sharing the mantra I use a whole helluva lot: "How we do the morning is how we do the day."

Three weeks later, Steve called to report that since we had spoken, he was getting up an hour before anyone else was stirring. He felt more focused and energized as he practiced mindfulness. During the day, he noticed that negative-thinking patterns and stress-based responses were less likely to hijack him. He was able to dependably regulate his emotions and calm his thoughts. As he came to welcome sitting quietly as the world woke up, he added a few things to his quiet time. Somedays he would read scripture. Other days he would journal. He was learning to meditate. He told me that grounding himself in stillness was helping him to accept constructive feedback. He was navigating organizational stressors, with optimism instead of skepticism.

His family appreciated the changes. He had time to have a cup of coffee with his wife before he left for the office. He made it a priority to check in with each of his three kids every morning before he switched his focus to work. In the evening, despite the conference calls still clamoring for his attention, he learned to be truly present during dinner and afterward, as he could. It amazed Steve that such a simple, inexpensive behavioral change would have such a powerful ripple effect.

Three years after he started the practice, Steve continues it every day—at home and on the road. It is an anchor and has improved his connection to himself, his spiritual life, his leadership, and his relationships.

The Ancient, Natural Need for Stillness

The power of listening deeply and of going still has been richly documented, steadily practiced, and quietly celebrated throughout all of history. In our modern-day world, noisy, overwhelming demands bombard us. Therefore, it is necessary that we cultivate a practice of stillness; we cannot listen to others if we do not listen to ourselves and are uncomfortable with stillness.

Stillness rocks. All great spiritual practices revere stillness. Going apart from the world. Being quiet. Setting an intention. A practice of restorative silence is at the core of spiritual growth and connection.

Psalm 46 says, "Be still and know that I am God." The New Testament talks about Jesus seeking solitary places to pray, enjoy solitude, refuel, and practice the wisdom of silence.

Silence is the basis of the Hindu practice of *mauna*; Mahatma Gandhi practiced silence every Monday, communicating only through writing.

At the center of Buddhism is the belief that one must aspire to quieting the mind, cultivating stillness, and achieving a clarity that allows one to see more clearly, create serenity, and be present, even in the midst of change and impermanence.

Silence can be found throughout the Jewish traditions and especially in Jewish mysticism. Ecclesiastes 3:7 said it best in referring to the fact that there is "a time to be silent and a time to speak."

Native American spirituality embraces the restorative power of silence as a way to connect with a larger, transcendent oneness:

> *Listen to the wind, it talks.*
> *Listen to the silence, it speaks.*
> *Listen to your heart, it knows.*[10]

Even the natural world honors stillness.

Winter, the introvert of seasons, is nature's way of going quiet to reenergize, to pull back, and to retreat from busyness into a nourishing rest. Additionally, many creatures hibernate to conserve energy and survive during times of depletion, cold, and food scarcity; these species often exhibit a deeper sense of wisdom than many human beings. We, too, need to rest, lean into the winters of our lives, and find ways to nourish ourselves not just during difficult times but daily.

By going still, we harness the insight and compassion needed to create our best lives, improve our self-awareness and, as a result, our connection to others. To lead with agility and focus instead of rigidity and distraction. To parent with presence. To explore what we feel, emotionally regulate, and communicate emotions in healthy ways. To deal with daily disappointments. To navigate the eruptions that come into all of our lives. To say "no" and set boundaries with compassion.

Only by being quiet can we hear the ancient source of wisdom that lives within us and tap into the natural order of things. Listening in the silence is an act of courage. It makes us vulnerable. Yet, in making us vulnerable, it can transform our experiences and relationships.

What Is Listening Deeply?

The previous chapter spoke about connecting consciously, which includes having a mindfulness practice that takes one deeper within; the idea of connecting consciously acknowledges that leadership is not about title or position, but it is about the leader's level of wellbeing.

Listening deeply is more specifically about the practice of mindfulness and embracing the reflective solitudes of our lives so we can be more present and connected to others—those we lead and those we love. Listening deeply is a mindset and heart-focus so we can foster in ourselves and give to others what we all want: to be heard, understood, and seen.

Listening to others can be hard. It is even harder if we don't learn to listen to ourselves. Many times, we are taught to reflect back, like a mirror, what a person says to demonstrate we have heard and understood them. That is a great place to start, but it is not enough. A mirror reflects an image flatly. You can repeat words but still not honor the heart of the speaker. And truth be told, this reflective listening can come across as condescending. "I hear you saying..." can sound stilted, forced, and redundant.

I think of listening as a prism, not a mirror. As opposed to simply reflecting back like a mirror, listening deeply serves as a prism by separating the white light—what the person is saying—into colors—feelings, thoughts, beliefs—that can be clearly witnessed and explored. Being a leader in the boardroom or the family room, means it is difficult to separate all the nuances of what someone is saying if we don't first practice with ourselves: we have to be able to sort through our feelings, our complex thought patterns, and our emotional patterns. Therefore, a meditation/mindfulness practice is essential in helping with this.

Listening deeply means absorbing, seeking to understand, and engaging with the speaker's words. As a result, listening deeply accomplishes several important things:

- It encourages the listener to identify and empathize with the feelings and ideas being expressed.
- It tunes in to what is not being said and what lurks beneath the surface.
- It encourages curiosity, which is the commitment to learning more.

Listening deeply is a way of life. It helps us pay attention to the gentle nudges of the spirit and leads us to embrace our purpose. It deepens relationships as people feel heard, seen, and supported. It clarifies meaning and intent; it is an essential leadership strategy that enhances the power of connection.

Listening deeply can happen on your porch. On quiet walks. In the doctor's office. In the classroom. In the elevator and on the airplane. It happens anywhere you are when you are mindful. It happens when we are present to each moment, breathing in what is happening around us and inside us. The painful moments. The elation. The defeats. The joys.

To give the gift of listening like a prism to a colleague, friend, or family member, one must first accept the varied topography of their own internal landscape. The eruptions. The messiness. The overflow. The beauty. The soul. And then share that acceptance with another.

So, how do we do this?

How to Listen Deeply

Let me start with a story about how not to listen. When our son Matthew was eight, I traveled to London on business, accompanied by him and my husband. The plan: they would play while I worked. My work entailed spending two days helping a team enhance its engagement. We were going to focus on how deepening the team members' self-awareness would improve their ability to listen, trust, connect, and perform as leaders. I had spent months working with the team's individual members prior to the team event. We were now ready to take the next step: working together in an open, compassionate way to enhance success.

Before I showed up at my client's corporate headquarters, I blew it with my son in the hotel room. He had only slept two hours on the flight across the Atlantic; he was sleep-deprived, jetlagged, out of his routine, and crabby. He was not the only one.

Instead of listening to his cues and words, I focused on talking, giving instructions, and lecturing. Instead of being with him and tuning in to his needs, I focused on doing—settling in, deciding on a place to eat, making sure I felt in charge—and talking to deal with my overwhelm and anxiety (a deeply entrenched pattern of mine). The more I tuned out and focused on my agenda, the more irritated he became. The more I talked at him in a demanding tone, the more upset he became. The more upset he became, the more controlling I became. We were a hot mess. It was on me.

Later that evening, I realized I had missed a royal opportunity to listen deeply. I had squandered a chance to just be with my son, extend compassion, and give him space to emotionally calm and physically rest. And I blew it because I did not hit my own pause button: in hindsight, I should have taken a few moments to practice mindfulness instead of focusing on unpacking and organizing and all the busyness that kept me in a highly alert state; if I had found a way to quiet my own inner noise, I would have been more able to breathe through the transition of time zone changes and dealing with the pre-day jitters that come before any major client engagement.

I teach this stuff! Yet, in that moment of hot-messiness, stillness evaded me. How different our relationship would have been that evening if I had shared what I was feeling, observing in him, and communicated my hopes for our evening and time in London. The emotionally healthy, empathetic mom would have said, "I know you are really tired (so am I), and you have done a great job travelling. I also feel a bit overwhelmed, and I have a big day tomorrow. Why don't you take a bath, and I'll fix us some tea? Then we can relax and, as a family, settle in and enjoy being together."

Instead, the exhausted, emotionally insensitive, anxious mom found ways to disconnect, blame, and stir up the irritation even more.

How many times do we do this with those who are most important to us? To those with whom we work closely nearly every day? Probably more often than we are even aware.

What would happen if more people in our workplaces and in our homes practiced silence every day? What would happen if, before each team meeting, everyone took a few deep breaths to prepare and focus, put their phones down, and did a quick mindfulness meditation? If each person had a practice of silence that would allow them to listen to their own thoughts and feelings uninterrupted, and as a result of this practice, were more apt to listen to others? To let others truly talk instead of jumping in as they take a breath? If we were less concerned with who was right and more focused on understanding and connecting? If we could show up like a steadfast oak tree, grounded and welcoming?

But how do you do that? Two friends recently manifested the fruits of practicing a meditative stillness when they came over on a day that I needed my community.

On this terrible, horrible, no good, very hard day Catherine called to say, "I am coming over. Bringing homemade soup. We can sit. You don't have to talk, but I am coming to be with you." While this devoted friend of mine dished out the potato and leek soup loaded with bacon and cheese her husband had made for us, I let myself be tended to—which is terrifying for me, because it means I have to admit I am out of gas and can't give to others. We sat. We ate. I hardly talked; I was out of gas, filled up with grief.

I did not even get out of my chair when it was time to load the dishwasher. I let Catherine do this, which, for me, is as monumental as humans walking on the moon. And then the doorbell rang, and the dogs went berserk, and I did not pop up to answer the door, and in walked Kelly, another friend to sit with us. And honestly, folks, if you knew me, you would have realized that my not getting up to serve or pour or answer or hug means I was truly, utterly humbled into a moment of sheer surrender and grace. For me to let others help and love and give means I must be getting this spiritual growth thing, just a little bit.

Both of my friends were able to be with me and create sacred space because of their own daily meditation and mindfulness practices. They read their inspirational literature. They attend services and meetings that fill their cup and help them to surrender to the power found in receiving. They pray...a lot. They are open to the wisdom found in simply being, rather than constantly doing. I was able to relax into doing nothing because they were able to be present. They did not come in with a flurry of activity. They were not chattering anxiously away. They did not make the moment about them. They knew what I needed. They came in doing God's work: helping to restore me to sanity—because they do the same for themselves.

We know the difference when we are in the presence of those who have a "listens deeply" practice. We breathe more easily. We feel emotionally safer. The entire vibe is less frenetic and more comfortable. I am thinking of a few recent times I was with people who don't have those practices; their anxious need to fill the silence with chatter and activity is enough to create a panic attack in a practicing Buddha.

Several practices encourage this kind of deep listening. Each are lifelong endeavors that help move us forward into a deeper rhythm with ourselves and others, whether it be at work or at home:

- **Stillness.** First and foremost, to be a kick-ass, world-class leader who listens to themselves and others, a daily practice of solitude and stillness is required. There is no shortcut. This practice grounds you, and that grounding will inspire others to cultivate their own practice of silence. If the hardest and most enriching work I do is on myself, then it stands to reason that to be a more effective leader, I benefit from being a more effective "me." Practicing stillness and mindfulness helps immensely.

- **Self-discovery.** We begin to know and accept ourselves more fully as a result of solitude, stillness, and mindfulness. To leverage our self-awareness and regulate our emotions in productive ways, we must identify what we are feeling. To learn what beliefs, attitudes, stinkin' thinkin', and woundedness lie underneath the surface emotion, and come to the table of emotional connectedness with an attitude of curiosity ("What else can I learn about myself?") and self-compassion ("How do I balance self-acceptance while gently nudging myself toward growth?"). What those of us in the leadership space know is that nothing (no degree, no title, no Learjet, no byline) trumps the power of self-discovery when it comes to sustainable professional and personal success.

- **Other-awareness.** Just as essential as self-discovery is the ability to tune in to others with empathy while simultaneously honoring yourself. This is the delicate balance of respecting the "I" while honoring the "you" and appreciating the "we." Sounds poetic and appealing. It is difficult and scary. Since we cannot do for others what we cannot do for ourselves, we benefit by developing a healthy relationship with ourselves: accepting who we are, being aware of our feelings, understanding our unhealthy thinking patterns that keep us stuck, and exhibiting rigorous self-honesty and accountability. It requires a quiet confidence, emotional regulation, an understanding of our limits and boundaries, and emotionally intelligent ways of communicating. Being tuned in to others essentially means you interact in a way so that others feel understood and respected even during times of conflict and differences; you can feel and accept their feelings because you are in tune with yours.

Impact of Stillness and Listening Deeply

At a recent two-day meeting with a CEO and his immediate team, we started each day off with five minutes of silence and guided meditation. Phones off. Laptops closed.

During those five minutes, I simply asked people to be aware of their thoughts, let them go, breathe deeply, and get in touch with the calmer side of themselves as they set an intention for the day. This was designed to allow people to experience the power of silence. Try to imagine a room full of mostly left-brain thinkers who fancy themselves movers and shakers and who don't come equipped with on-off switches, processing this suggestion of practicing stillness and intentional reflection. The eye-rolling and sighing were of Olympic proportions.

While everyone learned and shared much during those two days, participants reported that the five minutes of silence each day were invaluable. I was certainly not above saying, "I told you so." What they said about this forced-mindfulness included these things:

- "We get precious little of it in our culture."
- "We are not often invited to be 'nonproductive,' and sitting in silence is counter to the 'get-up and get-things-done' command."

Increasingly so, business leaders, along with many other influential thinkers, are coming forth to share their transformative experiences with silence and meditation. Benefits of the practice go beyond benefits achieved through other types of relaxation or exercise. Many well-regarded and successful business leaders report having a practice of daily reflection and stillness because they find it not only quiets their minds, it makes them a better leader, including Warren Buffet, Bill Ford, and Jeff Weiner. Moreover, a number of major companies, including Aetna, Google, AOL, and Apple, have started meditation and mindfulness programs for their employees.

The Wharton School of Business offers meditation classes to students striving to excel in this constantly plugged-in and talking world. Deloitte, the global consulting firm, has even created its own Meditation Series in conjunction with Emily Toner and offered on apps like Insight Timer and streaming platforms like SoundCloud.

So, there must be something to this! Research repeatedly indicates that practicing silence in the form of meditation improves cognition, productivity, empathy, emotional intelligence, listening, creativity, serenity, problem-solving, and attention. It lowers stress levels. When people meditate and invite these benefits into their workplaces, so much can improve.

Meditation helps children and families because it decreases stress, increases happiness, enhances stability, and lessens irritability. It helps people of all ages be better problem-solvers; accept impermanence and flow with change; and stabilize mood swings while increasing self-acceptance and empathy. It helps us relax instead of believing our only choices are fight or flight. It calms the nervous system, the organizational system, and the family system, even if just one person in the group practices it.

A study led by Harvard researchers at Massachusetts General Hospital found that meditating for only eight weeks significantly changed the brain's grey matter.[11] This is the part of the brain that processes information and provides energy and nutrients to neurons. As a result of this research, evidence shows that meditation can improve memory, sense of self, and empathy, while decreasing feelings of stress.

The practice of carving out solitude and committing to a practice of mindfulness and meditation does not mean we have one more thing "to work on." Meditation works on us if we allow it.

On the day I received my breast cancer diagnosis over the phone from my doctor, and after crying in a heap on the floor with my husband beside me, I joined my then-ten-year-old son by the pool where he was doing the day like a ten-year-old boy does, with not a care in the world. Such is the life of a momma; all I could think about was my supersized worries, especially as they related to how this life-threatening news would impact my boy, and how I was going to put one foot in front of the other, be there for my son, and deal with the terror spreading its way through every ounce of me. As I sat there watching Matthew swim, an insect landed on me. As I turned to swat the insect, Matthew said, "Mom, don't. That's a praying mantis."

I was tuned in enough, despite my skin-crawling fear and desperation, to realize that perhaps this was a sign of something. Imminent death perhaps? Or something else? I was rooting for the "something else."

As I researched the spiritual meaning of a praying mantis, I discovered the mantis is the garden-variety equivalent of a tremendous warrior who gains power through stillness. She focuses that power to lead, fight, and defend. I wanted to be the human version of a praying mantis, and while I had plenty of fight in me from the time I fell out of the womb, I wanted to do a better job connecting my fight with my inner calm.

From that day forward, I committed to—once again—rechanneling my power through the practice of stillness even more so. This is obviously, a reoccurring theme for me and a consistent invitation from the universe. And thankfully, this practice has brought me closer to myself and my loved ones. It has recharged my relationship with God. It has refocused my work and helped me lead my clients in new directions. It has reenergized me as I have stepped into complete health. It has allowed me to accept the challenging parts of my life, name them, and have the courage to change what I can change.

The praying mantis taught me to connect "fight" with "stillness." Curiously, many mornings as I went to my radiation treatments, a praying mantis landed on the window outside my bedroom. And on the one-year anniversary of my diagnosis, I found one sitting quietly on an outside bannister.

When we are tuned in to the world around us, we get inspiration and support from so many avenues. This support fortifies our journey as leaders and helps us to tap into the wisdom that exists all around us.

In the next chapter and beyond, we will discuss what is possible in professional and personal circles when we have the gifts of connecting consciously and listening deeply as cornerstones.

Connection Reflection for Strategy Two: Listens Deeply

o   How we do the morning is how we do the day. Develop a morning routine that allows you to sit quietly, breathe, reflect, and absorb the silence (I always do this over coffee). You can add in mindfulness, journaling, meditation reading, prayer, or Centering Prayer (a Christian meditation practice believed by some to have started with the Desert Fathers of early Christian monasticism while others trace it back to the Lectio Divina tradition of Benedictine monasticism). Find what works for you.

o   Allow yourself to be intentional about gratitude. Write down your gratitude list every day. Be present to each moment and purposeful about acknowledging all that is beautiful in your life.

o   Tune in to nature; there are many signs from the natural world that help us to find our way, deepen our connection, and elevate our energy.

o   Think of the ways you can bring a listening deeply practice to your workplace. Is there a meditation practice you can do at lunch time? Can you start each meeting you facilitate with an invitation to all attendees to breathe, to be with their feet are, and exhale?

Chapter Four

Exhibits Empathy: Enough, but Not Too Much

"If you can learn a simple trick, Scout, you'll get along a lot better with all kinds of folks. You never really understand a person until you consider things from his point of view... until you climb inside of his skin and walk around in it."
—Atticus Finch in *To Kill a Mockingbird* by Harper Lee

The radiation therapy was knocking me on my butt. An exhaustion accompanies radiation that defies all description we have for fatigue, and I am not often at a loss for words to describe much of anything. Day in and day out, I wanted to cry just thinking about going for my next treatment. On the other hand, by contrast, I also looked forward to going because I felt that nothing bad could happen as long as I kept doing so. It was a seesaw of desire balanced by weariness. Emotional terror joined with physical exhaustion. I had breast cancer—the same thing that killed my mother and my aunt. This predator had stalked me for years, and so I looked that horrific animal directly in the eye and was determined to leave victorious.

The magical, mystical spirits showed up: the prayers and kindnesses of many, an outpouring of supportive sentiments. This combination of fear—mine—and loving kindness—theirs—reminded me of one translation for the beginning of the medieval tale *The Grail Legend*: "Here begins your descent. Here begins the book of the Holy Grail. Here begin the terrors. Here begin the miracles."[12]

How many times do angels show up when the terror begins? How many moments are we brought to our knees, only to then witness angels marching in, flying in, dancing in…or silently waiting to be invited in? My angels showed up in many forms. They were loud and boisterous. Sacred and irreverent. Football-throwing and meal-bringing. Handholding and tissue-sharing.

My husband, son, brother, and cousins kept the vigil with me and offered healing reassurances. My friends listened to my fears and watched over Matthew so he could continue enjoying kid stuff. Then there were the prayer warriors: a combination of friends, family, colleagues, and strangers of such tremendous devotion that tears well up as I write this and think about them. All of these people stepped into my skin and walked around in it, like Atticus Finch encourages us to do.

One day, Matthew asked who was bringing dinner that evening. For weeks, dinners would mysteriously show up; it was planned serendipity. It was an old-fashioned, rooted-in-connection ritual I remember my grandmother, mother, and aunt doing for others: bringing food as a symbol of community, love, and healing. But we had no one bringing dinner that night, so I assured Matthew that we would eat and all would be well. No one had starved yet on my watch.

However, the magical, mystical spirits had other plans.

The doorbell rang at 4 p.m., and a waiter from one of our favorite restaurants appeared on the other side of the door with serving dish after serving dish of our favorite entrees. It was enough to feed a small country. Sandra, the exemplary executive assistant of a long-term client of mine, Bob, had orchestrated it. I knew they had much more to do than to think of me. Bob traveled the world and led his team. Sandra seemed to have more on her plate than even Bob did as she juggled so much for their organization. Yet, they had climbed into my skin and walked around in it. Needless to say, I cried, and my son was relieved that we had something to eat.

Six months later at an offsite meeting with Bob and his entire team, Jonathan, one of his young superstars, sat next to me. As I drank my ginger tea and mentioned how ginger was healing, we chatted, caught up, and agreed on how good it was for me to be getting stronger, working again, and connecting with my clients. These words of his stayed with me: "I am so glad you are sharing this with me." Three days later, the doorbell rang as my family and I were sitting down to dinner, prepared by me this time.

A large package sat on our porch, filled with ginger tea from Jonathan with a note that said, "To continued healing." He had quietly absorbed my comment and ran with it, demonstrating that his heart had heard me. I could see Atticus Finch smile.

Jonathan expressed his empathy when he said, "I am so glad you are sharing this with me." His empathy had moved him to action. Empathy in action is compassion. In this case, with enough ginger tea to drink for weeks, thanks to Jonathan, I felt understood and cared for.

Many, many moons later, during a time of deep, complex grief, another package showed up from the same Jonathan and his wife— this one from a luxurious bakery in New York City. It was filled with pastries and sweets, including a chocolate babka that would make the angels swoon. It was a reminder that some humans, like Jonathan, are empathy walking.

What Is Empathy?

Empathy is a big word these days. I like that we are talking about it, touting it, and encouraging its importance. Neuroscientists, developmental psychiatrists, songwriters, and business thought leaders extol the virtues of empathy, and rightly so. People need to know that others care before they open up and follow them. Like Theodore Roosevelt said, "No one cares how much you know, until they know how much you care."[13]

Empathy comes from the Greek words *em* ("in") and *pathos* ("feeling"). It literally means to be "in feeling" with another. As the theologian and writer C.S. Lewis once penned, "Friendship is born at that moment when one person says to another: 'What! You, too? I thought I was the only one.'"[14]

The way I see it, empathy is when you understand your own feelings *and*, as a result, can step into another's emotions. Empathy is the heart's mirror and reflects the inner world: theirs with ours. As true for all the seven strategies of connection, we cannot genuinely give what we don't have. Our ability to be "in feeling" with another is directly related to our ability to acknowledge, name, and be okay with the world of our own feelings.

Recently, my cousin, John, who is an Episcopal priest, gave a homily at a funeral. He spoke about the power found in gathering together to give witness to our grief and the importance of naming one's emotions:

> *"We give witness to other feelings as well. We gather to give witness to grief and whatever you are feeling … bring it today. I invite you to name it. Name it within yourself. Give witness to whatever you are feeling for it is true."*[15]

When we learn to acknowledge each feeling, we are moving toward a more awakened sense of emotional and spiritual wellbeing: important for those leaders who want to connect in more powerful ways to themselves and others. This connection is at the very core of feeling understood. It emerges in close relationships where trust abounds and vulnerability is the spoken language. Throughout our lives, including at work, we need this empathetic attunement to feel connected, enhance success, elevate a sense of purpose, and grow together.

Paul, an experienced and inspiring leader, shares the following,

> "There is this moment when you have to step into the shoes of another entire function, not just a person, whether it be operations or marketing or IT, and get

them to support your project. It most definitely requires a strong empathy muscle which, when I think about it, is more about how you say what you say. Sure, I need to know what other colleagues in the company are up against, how they are feeling, and what their goals are. That's a given but I have seen too many people go back to their offices and wonder why their brilliant presentation did not receive support. It is not because they had the wrong facts, or an incomplete argument. They failed by having the wrong delivery—the way they made their pitch lacked an emotional connection to their audience. Empathy is an art."

Since we are neurologically wired to connect, we are also more engaged and empowered at work and home when we know that others get us. In today's marketplace, executives look for ways to enhance engagement and empowerment. Who does not want an engaged, empowered workforce that enjoys work, performs at the top of their game, and behaves like a talent magnet? Nothing takes us all the way home, but empathy is a superpower when manifested in healthy ways; stay tuned for more on this.

Empathy Is Not for Everyone

As disappointing as it is, many are not willing or able to hone this great connecter called empathy. There are a number of reasons people may not want to journey deep inside themselves, expend the energy, and wrestle in the mud with themselves or with others:

It is too emotionally exacting and hard. Being empathetic requires connecting to your own jigsaw puzzle of emotions. Not everyone wants to look at those puzzle pieces and examine how they all fit. They look at the jumbled-up pieces and decide there is no easy place to start, it is too much work, it feels quite overwhelming—and why bother when there could be instantaneous gratification or distraction elsewhere?

Judgment takes over. Since being empathetic requires an emotional willingness, many will find it easier or more entertaining to find fault instead of acceptance. Many hold the misguided belief that judging someone means they can avoid being vulnerable themselves. Judgment is numbing, self-validating—and corrosive. It eats away at us and prevents us from looking at ourselves.

Empathy can be scary. Sitting with someone in the sacred space of empathy can be frightening. An awful lot of intimacy and intensity occurs when you are empathetic about someone's successes or their heartbreaks—just you, the other person, and feelings. It brings you close, creates vulnerability, jogs your memories about your own mistakes and pain, reminds you of how fragile life is, and moves you out from the protection of life's polite civilities. Holding sacred space creates rawness, not easy answers. That is the point. That is why it is so exquisitely powerful.

A client told me a story that was both frustrating and sad to hear. His mother was dying after a long illness. There was not much time left, and an estranged relative wanted to come and say her goodbyes. After a few days of reflection and checking with other trusted family, my client agreed to this relative's request in the hopes that it might bring some closure and healing. It was not long after the estranged relative arrived that a nurse suggested she leave.

The estranged relative was ill at ease and as anxious as a cat on a hot tin roof as soon as the visit got underway: talking incessantly, tapping her foot. My client's mother was in a comatose state and had been breathing calmly and steadily; she started to breathe in an agitated way when the relative started to talk. The relative—a cousin who had done some emotional damage to my client's mother, and who had had no healthy connection to the dying woman for years—was oblivious to the impact her presence was having on the dying woman's wellbeing. She chattered away, reliving memories from forty years earlier, memories my client said his mother was not interested in recounting when she was alert and healthy. This visit, though seemingly intended as an opportunity to apologize to the dying woman, was really all about the cousin's anxiety and her desire for absolution.

There was nothing remotely empathetic and connected about this person's presence, and she was not tuned in enough to realize how her behavior was affecting my client's mother. She showed up in the room of the dying without empathy, filling the space with her anxiety and selfish agenda.

She left when the nurse asked her to, still clueless about the emotional state her presence had created. Just a few minutes after her departure, my client's mother calmed down. Her breathing slowed and returned to an easy pace.

Even those dying, and in a coma, respond to the emotions of those around them. So what does that mean for the rest of us? It means we tremendously impact and are impacted by those around us.

Empathy and Its Gifts

A recent guest on Jacob Morgan's podcast, *The Future of Work*, Kimberly Samon said this when asked her about the role empathy plays in her leadership: "We can't be good leaders if we're not good listeners. Whether someone is talking about the struggles they're having with a project or the struggles they're having at home, which might flow over into work and wanting to be mindful of that, listening is absolute table stakes."[16]

Empathy – supported by the cornerstone of listening deeply - is an investment that yields priceless returns. Look at these champions of empathy to understand why it is a leadership superpower:

- Joann S. Lublin reports in *The Wall Street Journal* that companies such as Cisco Systems, Incorporated and Ford Motor Company are among the 20 percent of American companies putting managers through empathy training to produce better managers and happier employees.[17]

- According to the State of Workplace Empathy Report, 72 percent of CEOs surveyed believe that workplace empathy drives financial benefits in the form of better performance and even business growth.[18]

- "In addition to confidence, a CEO must have empathy, Satya Nadella, CEO of Microsoft, says. This is a quality one doesn't typically see on a list of top CEO character traits. But in Nadella's view, empathy is, among other things, a key source of business innovation. He says that although many regard it as a "soft skill," not especially relevant to the "hard work of business," it is a wellspring for innovation, because innovation comes from one's ability to grasp customers' unmet, unarticulated needs."[19]

- In their article, "The CEO Moment: Leadership for a New Era," Carolyn Dewar et. al. discuss the importance of showing up with our best, most empathetic selves in order to be leaders who are present and fully human.[20]

Empathy requires bravery; it scoffs at anything less. Journeying into our inner world of feelings can be a painful excursion, but it is what allows us leaders to create cultures of abundance and connection instead of scarcity and fear. It can be hard to revisit our personal vulnerability or remorse when we are reminded of it through the experiences of another. Yet, we can also relive our high points through the successes of another, which can make us feel content and open-hearted. These shared experiences—the tough ones and the joyful ones—tap into the healing power of empathy and form a collective story which:

- Strengthens trust and intimacy.
- Creates an emotionally safe place in which people can thrive.
- Encourages emotional honesty and openness.
- Gives hope by encouraging resilience.
- Breaks through shame and isolation.
- Invites collaboration.

- Creates a greater sense of self-esteem, courage, and purpose.

Let's turn yet again to Nadella, who, through his own life experiences, has strengthened his own capacity to demonstrate empathy. In a recent CNBC interview, he admits that he was not always empathetic. He sees empathy, now that he has developed it in himself, as a critical component not just for personal wellbeing but also in business: "[With] every passing mistake you make, you develop more of a sense of being able to see life through other people's eyes." Empathy, he argues, can "make you a more effective parent, more effective colleague and a more effective partner…. Most people think empathy is just something that you reserve for your life and your family and your friends, but the reality is that it's an existential priority of a business."[21]

From Buzzword to Superpower

Empathy is a pretty popular word nowadays. That is a good thing, but it is also concerning: organizations can't create empathy just by telling their people to be empathetic (which is often what happens) or sending them to a workshop (which may be well-intentioned, but is not enough). This oversimplistic notion of how to cultivate and employ empathy cheapens the concept of empathy until it becomes a buzzword, overused, and abused.

It will take consistent effort to turn "empathy" from a buzzword into a superpower. We don't wave a wand, send our people to a training seminar, watch a YouTube video, and automatically become empathetic. Empathy is a lifelong journey that starts and stops with our own emotional, spiritual, mental, and relational vulnerability which strengthens our wholeness.

Here are three truths to keep in mind that further emphasize why empathy is hard to master and why it is so important for leadership:

1. **We have to first show ourselves empathy.** We can't give what we don't have. We can't teach what we are not also learning.

If we judge ourselves unfairly, shame ourselves, and do not give voice to our emotional life, we are not able to create a safe place for our employees; we have to close the escape hatches of shame and blame, gossip and judgment if we are to help others grow. We must be okay with us. It is empowering when we stop hustling for approval and draining our own energy by giving it away when we have none for ourselves. Slowing down, naming our emotions, and self-reflecting on an ongoing basis fills our cups with self-acceptance, forgiveness, and compassion. Then, and only then, can we begin to consistently show empathy to others.

2. **Empathy is triggering.** When we sit with someone else's pain, it can activate our own grief, stress, vulnerability, and whatever else the three-ring circus that is our emotional life can throw at us. This is more than okay; when our emotions get activated, we become more authentic, which helps us to live with the feelings instead of denying them or letting them run the show. The more we name and accept our feelings, the less we are triggered or hijacked by them. Emotions are messages; we can pay attention to what they are communicating, but we do not have to set up camp and live in them. To be comfortable with our emotions, we practice being so. This is even more reason to embark on that process of self-discovery—so we have the emotional reserves and resilience to draw from when we are listening to someone's overwhelm and struggles, joy and pain.

3. **Empathy needs boundaries.** Consistent and respectful boundaries are key if, as leaders at work and in life, we want to show up without stepping out of our lane. If we have too much empathy, we aim to fix others when they are hurting or stressed instead of providing a safe container. If we have too much empathy, we take responsibility when it is not ours to take (there have been times in my life I have felt responsible for world hunger). When there are no boundaries to our empathy, we are more likely to try and find a solution when it is not our

problem or try to cheer others' up because we are uncomfortable with their struggles. We sometimes mistake empathy for making excuses for our employees, colleagues, or loved ones instead of holding them accountable for their decisions so that they can learn to trust that they can find the solution. Boundaries must ride shotgun with empathy to prevent us from becoming "empathyholics," who, in turn, prevent others from discovering their own strength, courage, and wisdom. Boundaries honor our space while conveying we trust others to navigate their own storm, find a safe harbor, and realize the waves, strong as they are, will not overtake them.

Though empathy is hard, as evidenced by how complicated the above three guidelines can be, it is worth the effort. So, I offer these six reminders, because connection is not microwaveable and empathy is not instantaneous:

1. **Empathy is a state of mind.** For empathy to be authentic, leaders have to truly care about what their people are going through. You can't script empathy. It does not happen because one attends a training or reads an article. It is a way of life that sprouts from the deep roots of self-connection.
2. **Empathy is silent.** In order for empathy to be most powerful, leaders have to forego their desire to fix, lecture, and advise. Tune in and listen up; put away your map, playbook, and list. Stop with the "have you thought about this?" Give some space so that those around you can process their own emotions and share their story.
3. **Empathy is generous.** When someone shares their story, it is not time to jump in with yours; do not hijack the conversation and put the focus on you. Listen deeply and give yourself generously to the moment.

4. **Empathy is feeling-based.** Share what you are feeling as a result of someone's experience. They will appreciate that you cared enough to be emotionally impacted.

5. **Empathy is wise.** Let the other person have their experience. By doing so, you communicate your faith that they have what it takes to rise up, learn from the situation and their emotions, and step into their true self.

6. **Empathy is grateful.** When someone shares their story, it gets woven in with yours and deepens the connection. Thank them for opening up to you and be aware of the fact that even if there are no words to capture the moment, expressing gratitude is powerful.

Empathy creates empathy. It is contagious. It enhances empowerment, gives hope, builds trust, and strengthens resilience. It contributes to an emotionally healthy work culture that allows for growth, learning, and risk-taking while encouraging accountability. It feeds the soul, and we need more soul at work as more companies realize that having empathetic leaders enhances trust, productivity, engagement, and even financial performance.

Empathy is the right thing to lead with, even without the positive impact on metrics. To connect, we have to show up fully human, ready to step into the shoes of another and, when it is our turn, invite someone to step into ours.

Empathy Begins at Home

Yet empathy is not a magic potion. We have to tread lightly, be careful, and not give it too much power while also recognizing its meaningful tonic. As with everything, there must be moderation, balance, and a careful examination.

I don't want to be a killjoy. I am a huge fan of empathy, but I have experienced the downside of it too. When people are overly empathic to others without having boundaries, it can become a version of McEmpathy: driving through for a quick fix. When this happens and the sole focus is to make someone else feel better without regard for your own wellbeing, or you give it so you can feel comfortable or worthy, it is not empathy: it is manipulation and self-serving.

This is how this works: if we are not showing ourselves empathy, if we do not have clear boundaries, if we think we should rush in to cheer someone up, it becomes about us. It might be covered up in "look how thoughtful I am being," but if our actions are rooted in our need to be needed, then we are trying to manipulate the situation to make ourselves feel powerful or indispensable or less anxious. Eventually, this kind of interaction leaves everyone involved kind of queasy, uneasy, and depleted.

Let's clear up a few misconceptions about empathy and the compassionate actions that spring from it. Being empathetic and demonstrating compassion does not mean you:

- Let people walk all over you.
- Say "yes" to everything and everyone.
- Sacrifice yourself to please someone else.
- Allow yourself to be overwhelmed by another's feelings.
- Rescue someone or fix his or her problem.
- Let someone else's pain change what you need to be safe.

Empathy fatigue takes a toll when boundaries are nonexistent as a result of over-caring for someone else and not taking care of ourselves. Since I am a recovering "empathyholic," I can speak to what empathy fatigue looks like:

- In the face of pain that belongs to someone else, you set up camp and move in, instead of visiting and establishing sacred space.
- Their pain becomes your pain; their descent into hell, yours.
- Their life becomes your life, and it is difficult to focus on your priorities and feelings as you become flooded with theirs.

- Their victories are your complete pleasure.
- You wind up pissed off, resentful, and polishing your martyr trophy while everyone around you is feeling great and whistling.

The more naturally empathetic you are, the more you need to watch for these dangers.

I can feel people's emotions so quickly that large crowds can drain me. The degree of empathy and compassion I have are gifts. Yet, there were times when these gifts, left unchecked, could be disastrous for me until I learned to pace myself, ensure I was fueling myself, and keep distance from folks who are emotionally damaging for me—and still, I struggle. I had to learn that "no" is a complete sentence and that it is okay to move toward the joy and away from the soul-sucking takers.

I have spent a lot of time and reflection figuring out how to be empathetic without putting myself at risk. It is a lesson I work on every day, making sure the runaway trains don't crash at my station, even when I feel like I should flag them down. I have worked hard for the tempering wisdom I have now when it comes to how to channel my empathy, and it is not a lesson perfectly applied. I still work daily on accepting my own powerlessness and tuning in to a Higher Power instead of believing I am a higher power.

Connected Leaders must remind themselves that as they care for their people, their tribe, their employees, and their loved-like-crazy ones, the most courageous work they do is still on themselves.

The ABCs of Empathy

Often, people who have suffered are more apt to be empathetic. That makes sense, because rebuilding our own lives after crisis inspires us to want to help others find their way through the maze as well. This is not an easy life; it brings us face to face with immeasurable loss and doubt, and empathy plays a starring role in our stories of redemption and renewal.

We can all use tips—even those of us who fell out of the womb with a strong empathy muscle—so I created a mnemonic device to remind us how to demonstrate empathy regardless of the situation:

E mote   (tune into *your* emotions)
M indful   (be aware of your feelings and where your feet are)
P ause   (be still, listen, embrace the silence)
A ccept   (allow your feelings and the feelings of the other person)
T enderness   (have your tone and expressions reflect calmness)
H ealing   (focus on being a comforting presence)
Y ourself   (learn more about who you are)

These are some examples of what empathy sounds like when someone is suffering:

- "That is so very difficult."
- "I know how this feels; I want to hear more about your experience though."
- "Let's sit down so I can give you my undivided attention and put my phone on silent."
- "I can see how painful this is."
- "Tell me more."
- "Honestly, I don't have any words. I am really grateful you are telling me this."
- This is what empathy sounds like when someone is celebrating:
- "You've got to be so happy."
- "You've worked so hard. This is amazing!"
- "Let's go and celebrate you."
- "I can only imagine how relieved you feel."

Truth be told, some people are clueless about how to be empathetic, and others are terminal jerks, uninterested in digging deep into themselves to seed and nourish genuine empathy. These are some of the things that people might say that do not demonstrate empathy:

- "Everything happens for a reason."
- "Oh, what a shame."
- "Poor thing."
- "It will get better, you just need to _____."
- "God has a plan."
- "I know exactly how you feel." (Note: most likely, they don't. And even if they do, it is about turning the attention to them.)
- "I remember when..." and they launch into their own sob story; I call this emotional bait-and-switch.

People gravitate to those who know how to empathize. Many distance themselves from those who don't: the energy vampires who leave us feeling depleted and drained. Don't stay close to the vampires. And don't be one of these. Move toward those whose presence adds a positive impact and who fuel your energy in healthy ways. Become one who others turn to.

Recently, I took a call from the wife of a client. We chatted a little bit, and then she said, "I just want to thank you. I know you've been working with my husband on his leadership, and whatever you have been teaching him, we see the benefit at home. He expresses his emotions calmly, and not just anger. It used to be just anger. Now, we see all emotions. He spends time reflecting so he understands himself better. He is lighter, more at ease. He can really hear us now. And wants to understand what we are going through. He doesn't just offer advice or try to fix things. Now, he listens to how we feel without jumping in to make us feel better or force a solution. We actually want to be around him more."

This is empathy walking.

Connection Reflection for Strategy Three:
Exhibits Empathy

o All the connection strategies must start with ourselves before we can genuinely demonstrate them in sustainable and healthy ways to others. Be aware of how you talk to yourself and transform that self-talk to include encouraging, empathetic messages: "I made a mistake, and I am also loveable." "It is okay to rest when I am feeling depleted." "Taking a break is essential in order for me to show up with my best."

o Find some ways to show yourself compassion: make yourself a cup of tea, get plenty of sleep, be around people who care about you, be out in nature, exercise, eat nourishing food.

o Expand your empathy repertoire: send an old-fashioned card to someone instead of liking their social media posts, call a colleague just to check in, spend time with a friend, drop off a meal to someone who might need it, pray for someone. Each day be intentional about doing at least one extra empathy-related, connection-building activity.

o At work and at home, be willing to talk about how you are gentle and supportive of yourself when you make a mistake, or when you are feeling overwhelmed, or need time to do something fun. Be truthful about your story; find ways to show up perfectly imperfect, real, and fully human.

Chapter Five

Celebrates Curiosity: A True Superpower

"I believe that curiosity is the secret. Curiosity is the truth and the way of creative living. Curiosity is the alpha and the omega, the beginning and the end. Furthermore, curiosity is accessible to everyone."

—Elizabeth Gilbert

The Power of Curiosity

"We are not understanding each other...." Meg's words immediately got my attention. She was describing the dynamic among her team members, some of whom worked in the United States. Some in Asia. Others in Europe. "And it is not the cultural differences as much as we don't really know each other," she continued.

Over six months, the engagement scores in her organization dropped by 20 percent. Her boss, the CEO of this global enterprise, asked her to fix it. Many businesses use engagement to gauge the degree to which employees are invested in their companies. Engaged employees are passionate, committed, and motivated. They enjoy what they do and with whom they work. While they are not Pollyannas, they are constructive in their approach. They inspire others and show up to work with energy, optimism, and appreciation. Engagement impacts overall wellbeing.

Numerous elements impact the level of one's engagement. They include the degree to which your boss cares about you, trust, communication, having opportunities to develop, working with clear expectations, understanding a well-defined strategy, and honest yet empathetic leadership. Engagement is further positively impacted if one's boss actively understands through his/her actions that your personal life needs time and nourishment.

Engagement is usually measured through a company-wide survey, and yet what I have been telling my clients for years is this: a survey is not a strategy! Disseminating a survey is not the same as providing leaders with the tools, based in self-understanding, that will enhance engagement in sustainable ways. Remember that information is not transformation; data and analytics do not alone make a successful approach. Transformation only occurs when there is a deep, meaningful shift inside of the individuals who lead; this is what creates a groundswell of change.

While surveys provide an important snapshot of critical data, the real treasure is in finding the answer to this question: What are we going to do—to enhance engagement on a daily basis, people? Nothing changes if nothing changes, and changes must start with each individual leader having a personal awakening.

And it was this conundrum that I walked into when I had lunch with Meg after she had heard about my work on connection and leadership.

"How can I fix this? I don't even know where to begin. As I was asking myself this, I heard about you—that you have a unique approach more focused on the psychological, human pieces of engagement," she told me over Cobb salads.

Meg's mind was racing, trying to approach this problem like she would tackle most of her business challenges. She was known across the industry as a star, whose innovative and analytical mind shone through in everything she and her team did. She saw this engagement challenge as another problem to squash, check off her list, move on from, and tell her boss, "Look—I did good."

We chatted about her team, and I shared stories from my experience. She wove in stories from her life. The more we shared, the more she relaxed. The more she relaxed, the more reflective she became. Yet, she still did not know how to fix her situation.

"What would happen," I said, "if we just accepted the 'not knowing at this point' and instead just got real curious?"

Then, I carefully ventured, "Look, knowing is overrated. When we assume we know something, we don't venture any further, dig deeper, or ask questions. When we're married to 'knowing,' we overlook curiosity. Curiosity is where it's at! What would happen if you agreed to embarking on an exercise of curiosity? I can't promise what we would discover, but I can promise you we will unearth something important and perspective-changing."

Just nine months later, there was reason to celebrate. Not only did Meg and her team turn around their engagement scores, a much more satisfying sense of connection among team members resulted, too. Their engagement scores were at the top of her company's rankings, and colleagues were asking her how she and her team had accomplished that.

Meg was a bit sheepish as we talked over our celebration dinner. We had learned a lot about her and her team over the months we had worked together, and she was still remarking about how her initial approach—finding the problem and squashing it—was somewhat misdirected. She had wanted to send people to trainings, have consultants come in to talk about trust, and identify what was wrong in the culture. She was not thinking that the individuals on her team—her included—needed to dive deep into their own emotional and relational patterns.

When we first partnered with Meg and her team, her team members clearly did not relate to themselves *and* each other in ways that would build connection. There was an overall sense of disconnection: no meaningful self-awareness that was creating change, no empathetic conversations, no true understanding of each other's strengths, no real appreciation, and no guidelines to encourage healthy behavior while discouraging unhealthy behavior. Of course, there was minimal trust and precious little accountability.

As if that was not enough, people did not fully understand how their work linked to the overall strategy and goals of the business. They felt out of the loop; communication was sometimes helpful, sometimes nonexistent. Their input was not consistently asked for. Folks were indecisive and avoided tough conversations. Gossip was rampant as was the one-two punch of blame-and-shame. Expectations were unclear. Feedback was not given frequently enough. All this came together to create an environment of disengagement even though the team's performance was certainly "good enough."

While Meg's team was made up of generally kind human beings, they were so distracted by the relentless nature of their work that they forgot to prioritize creating an environment in which employees felt known, supported, inspired, and lifted up. And they had no idea that to create this kind of culture they would each have to commit to a rigorous self-discovery process. Like with so many executive teams, their daily business transactions superseded connected interactions.

Over nine months, through carefully laid out interventions and exercises, we helped Meg's team better understand their strengths, challenges, and areas that could be improved. We helped them get curious about themselves and each other through a process that included individual coaching and a deep dive into self-discovery; as with any cultural transformation done with connection as its anchor, it was not for the fainthearted.

Meg and her team worked courageously on developing their muscles of self-discovery. They rolled up their sleeves to do the hard work of true transformation and engagement: starting with shining the light on their blind spots so they could become more aware of the havoc they wreak. They focused on utilizing their strengths in evolved ways and becoming more adept at identifying when they were being driven by their narrow agendas or their fearful egos. They became more curious about how their default settings and embedded patterns were getting in the way of their performance and connections with others. It was not easy. Some resisted the process. Some embraced the learnings. All struggled—as us humans do—with putting down the control mechanisms that had ruled their interactions and thinking. However, many on Meg's team—Meg included—came to believe that parking their emotional life at the office door had hidden costs because these emotions and patterns leaked out at work.

As their curiosity grew, they learned things about themselves that helped them understand how they came across to others, what was positively impactful, and what got in their way of creating more harmonious, effective relationships. They learned to ask their colleagues questions that encouraged openness: "How did you feel after that meeting?" "Is there a way I can help you?" "I am struggling with something. Have time to chat?" "Can I give you some feedback?" Instead of just scratching the surface of facts, they slowly moved into peeling back the layers so they understood each other from an emotional, relational level.

The more they shared about themselves, the more they knew about each other. As the team learned to communicate more directly, frequently, and respectfully, it went from guarded and defensive to open and receptive. As with all of us beings who are attending human school, they had to learn to put aside the typical derailers like gossip and blame, competition and judgment. They learned to lift each other up instead of elevating themselves. As a result of getting curious about themselves and each other, they also became more willing to ask questions about the work, to show up "not knowing" so they could discover what might truly make an innovative difference.

In addition to individual evolution and growth, they began to create an emotionally safe environment so curiosity could thrive and the team could experience a revolution. Simply stated, humans are not going to open their hearts and share their thoughts if they do not feel safe to do so. To create an emotionally safe environment for Meg's team, guidelines were put in place that were taken very seriously, including the following:

- Growth and leadership start with yourself—practice learning how to stay honest, open, and willing.
- Confidentiality is non-negotiable (i.e., what is talked about here stays here).
- No talking about anyone else if they are not in the room (no gossip).
- Empathy is a must, and it starts with self-awareness.
- Omit language or tone that smacks of bullying (e.g., degrading, threatening).
- No blame and shame.

Many of us, myself included, review this list of emotional safety guidelines and think, *Surely, this does not apply to me. Those are for the mean people.* But, without fail, the more we explore how to specifically create emotionally safe environments, people become jaw-droppingly stunned as they realize, *I* am *the mean person.*

In the service of ratting myself out, I was one of those "kind" people who had to accept that I could be mean when feeling unsafe, overwhelmed, threatened, disrespected, and scared. We all experience times when we are "that" person who does things and interacts in ways that causes damage by saying a snarky comment, rolling our eyes, raising our voice; we all find ourselves in a primitive state when we feel threatened or traumatized and, as a result, behave like the kids in *The Lord of the Flies.*

Curiosity turns our attention to the defects we have normalized and that, in turn, create dysfunctional, demoralizing patterns at work and home. Once we are willing to accept that some of what we do adds to the less-than-ideal circumstances around us, the more apt we are, as leaders, to help others do the same and thrive.

Creating emotional, contractual guidelines like Meg's team did has a remarkably positive impact. Of course, there are always mishaps on the road to true understanding; it can be a struggle to stop the gossiping or the blaming of others. It takes a while to change behavior so that it becomes more of a habit as if it is part of our DNA.

There were also clear consequences put in place for people who did not respect what the team was trying to achieve. Some folks had to meet one-on-one with Meg so they could more clearly understand what was at stake, and how she wanted them to personally experience the uplift from this evolutionary kind of work. One was asked to take a break from coming to the office for two days and spend the time reflecting on whether or not she wanted to go on this journey, since her behavior continued to be sabotaging of others. Out of Meg's eight direct reports, only one decided this process was not going to work for him; he was able to be honest and had a direct conversation with Meg. He transitioned out of the organization, and that departure elevated the team culture even more positively.

Rejection is often protection; remember that.

And often times, when someone self-selects out of a new way of living and leading, they can still have an awakening as they move through their life. The seeds have been planted; they have been exposed to something new.

A year after we embarked on our "journey of curiosity," Meg's team revamped its strategies to support its growth in the marketplace. Enhancing engagement enhances performance. As the team's curiosity about themselves and each other took stronger root, it broke through the soil and gave bloom to work that, naturally, became more innovative and effective. Mistakes were now viewed as valuable lessons, so the team's fear around being wrong significantly lessened and gave way to inspiration.

As Meg said to me recently, "Who would have thought that curiosity would have made us more engaged and more successful?" The truth is, I did.

Curiosity and Engagement

When people are not curious and mindful about who they are, they spend much of their energy resisting the very thing that could set them free. What we resist most definitely persists. The linkage between connecting consciously, listening deeply, exhibiting empathy, and celebrating curiosity is strong. They all work together to positively activate our connection wiring.

This ability to be mindful and curious, empathetic and connecting, enhances our capacity for joy and true empowerment as we move away from the patterns that keep us thinking, mistakenly, that we are in control. This self-discovery-based curiosity, balanced by self-compassion and acceptance, also yields information we can use to improve the quality of our relationships with ourselves and those with whom we work and share our lives. This curiosity teaches us how to navigate relationships and situations in emotionally whole ways while opening us up to the power of spirituality in our lives.

So how do we get curious in a way that positively impacts our leadership? There is a way forward that builds on the practices of connecting consciously, listening deeply, and exhibiting empathy.

Let's start by discussing the benefits of curiosity for…well, curiosity's sake.

The Benefits of Curiosity

If stillness rocks, as we said previously, then curiosity empowers. It empowers us to know more about ourselves. It empowers us to dig deeper so we can harvest more in our relationships. It nudges us to do the hard work of discovering and embracing our purpose. It gets us in touch with the sacred, because when we are curious, we are more mindful of the small and big blessings and miracles around us.

Sacred awe requires, most certainly, a combination of mindfulness and curiosity.

So, here is the deal with curiosity. It is one powerful way to enhance connection, even as it stretches us and makes us uncomfortable. Its power is unsung, however, because we tend to live in a world that celebrates knowing. Curiosity is fueled by humility; it requires accepting our imperfections and surrendering to the fact that we do not know everything and can't control much of anything.

In our much younger years, most of us have a natural curiosity that can be unsettling for those in authority. As we get older, we lose it, because many of our cultural institutions systematically eradicate it. Many organized religions shame those who ask questions, even though many of the great spiritual leaders questioned the way things were done and shook things up. More than a few families are based on the notion that "Father and Mother know best," discouraging honest dialogue and a celebration of personal agency. Schools, to keep order, do not truly teach critical thinking: from elementary school through college, more classroom experiences are defined by staying in the box, coloring within the lines, and agreeing with the standard, promoted way than celebrating true discovery and difference of opinion. Sadly, this is becoming more—not less—true.

Sir Ken Robinson's TED Talk "Do Schools Kill Creativity?" is widely acclaimed.[22] His major premise: We don't live up to our potential because we are educated to behave, be dutiful, sit in our seats, accept authority, worship grades, and cultivate perfection. We stigmatize children and teens with curious minds and lots of energy. Many children and teens are afraid of making mistakes and are often shamed into silence as opposed to being alive with questions.

Some of the most curious children turn out to be lifelong learners when we encourage their curiosity and ensure their questions are celebrated. When we encourage curiosity, we have more than a fighting chance of raising kids who are alive in the moment, as opposed to just trying to jump through the next hoop.

It is the most curious adults that change our world. Take Steve Jobs, cofounder of Apple. Consider the business models for Amazon and Airbnb. Think of all the times you have simply said to friends,

"How in the world did someone think of that?" Yet, once the innovator's thinking brought something remarkable to fruition, the connecting of the dots seemed so effortless and simple. Why? Because embedded in curiosity is an intuitive wisdom: Curiosity connects not just the dots, but us!

Curiosity in the Real World

Brian Grazer has moved us to emotional heights through his work, which includes movies like *Parenthood, A Beautiful Mind, Apollo 13,* and his TV sensation, *Empire.* While Grazer is obviously gifted, he gives most of the credit to his endless curiosity, like Einstein does in his famous quote, "I have no special talents. I am just passionately curious."[23] In his book *A Curious Mind: The Secret to a Bigger Life,* Grazer simply says, "Curiosity can add zest to your life, and it can take you way beyond zest—it can enrich your whole sense of security, confidence, and well-being."[24] Interestingly, he credits his curiosity for enhancing nearly everything in his life, including how he leads others.

So I ask you this: Don't you want to be on the team of folks who rise every day to learn something new? Don't you want to be someone who turns an ordinary day into an adventure because you wonder, reflect, pursue, and appreciate? Isn't it exciting to be surrounded by people who are willing to awaken and heal because they want to learn everything they can in human school, including how to forgive and let go?

It takes courage, along with curiosity, to do new things, because there is a strong pull toward the safety and familiarity of the old. We are a culture that numbs out, often by watching our screens (an awful lot) or eating our feelings (don't you wonder why Oreos, which are not even food, are so popular?).

To be curious, let go of a few things: the desire to be right, the fear of failure, the comfort of the known, the relentless fight for control, and the search for perfectionism.

If we let go of all of that, then what is left? To what do we anchor ourselves? If we have to let go of all that to be truly present, whether in a strategic planning session or in a discussion with our high school junior about college, then how do we navigate the future?

Despite how scary it might feel to let go of the need for certainty, curiosity helps us embrace the power in the unknown. It gives us permission to question everything: ourselves, the way our families behave, religious beliefs, business models, and our rules of engagement. It is scary to ride the wave of curiosity. Yet, riding that wave can bring us to a new beachhead:

- Curiosity allows people to better manage complexity in the workplace with less stress. Putting down the need to be all-knowing and approaching a situation with openness takes the pressure off and creates a problem-solving, innovative atmosphere.
- Curiosity helps resolve conflicts, because we realize there is something far more valuable than being right. Acknowledging another person's point of view strengthens the relationship and does not mean, necessarily, that you agree. Curiosity has to be a two-way street, however, for it to be most effective for the relationship.
- Curiosity enhances positive energy, which in turn deepens emotional connection. Competitive mindsets, a focus on getting one's way, and sanctimonious attitudes rob us of the collaborative connection for which we are wired. Conversations turn into competitive sparring matches as the "weapons" of facts and statistics fly around, coupled with the competition-comparison two-step. There is nothing wrong with facts or statistics. And we have to blend our rational and emotional minds, thereby creating a wise mind focused on being innovative, connected, and willing to experience the whole hot mess.

Curiosity and Leadership

Leaders who practice curiosity are open, vulnerable, and transparent. Curious leaders, whether they are a teen leading a hiking expedition, a new CEO making decisions about reorganizing the enterprise, or a parent listening to a child's social dilemma do the following:

- They listen deeply and are present—they come to a conversation with an open attitude, not a defensive posture or self-validating argument. They put down the weapons of blame and shame. They focus on learning more.
- They ask empowering questions and are adept at getting people to tell them more.
- They laugh at themselves, are honest about their mistakes, and are okay about being wrong.
- They realize that saying "I don't know" is an act of self-confidence.
- They are resilient and have grit. They understand that failure is often the beginning of something more gratifying and empowering, that closing doors take us down a better hallway. They don't let past mistakes, or hurt, or disappointment become a life sentence. They get up, get going, get support, and get flourishing.

Us human beings are complex creatures, walking contradictions as we navigate this life. After one particularly tough year of self-reflection, during which I was really broken open, I admitted to God, myself, and my ride-or-die-tribe that some of my parenting had wounded our son. Needless to say, this admission created a huge outpouring of grief inside of me. I experienced an emotional and spiritual breakdown, fueled by my need to understand what I could change. I had to own how my anxiety and fear had contributed to heartache. Because of my desire to fix and rescue instead of connect and be curious, I had made mistakes as a mother.

It is hard to sit with this, even now as I write it.

While I was focused on fixing and rescuing my son along with mapping out his path, I was also unintentionally discouraging, disempowering, shaming, and damaging him. I was the great air-traffic-control-mom orchestrating and lecturing, creating and managing. I often gave Matthew space to make his own decisions, but I stepped in to rescue him instead of letting him live with the consequences. I was an emotional fuel tank, an ATM, a chronically-dispensing vending machine. And while I was really into control to assuage my own anxiety, I did not stick with the consequences; I had too much empathy for the struggle. It was way too much control and not enough of a safe container.

It was a mess I created based on my own fear and wanting to protect him from experiencing the same poverty and emotional scarcity I grew up with. I was obsessed with Matthew's life; I wanted him to know I had his back and understood. Yet, I had to figure out a different way and trust that the combination of letting go and having clear boundaries would allow he and I to enjoy—more consistently, honestly, and lovingly—our deep connection.

So…I went back to Step One in the Twelve Steps of recovery, which is the only step we have to do perfectly; it is about accepting our powerlessness and admitting how our thinking and behaviors have created a tsunami of unmanageability. I had to admit that, in many ways, I was addicted to making my son "happy," and that such a misguided obsession was damaging him, me, and our relationship. My love for him made me tremendously vulnerable (how could I survive ever losing him in any way?), and yet I surrendered: no amount of controlling him would make me feel less vulnerable. I needed to realize that the joy I feel having him in my life was a one day at a time experience and that all of my love would not keep him safe. Lord have mercy, I had to entrust my son to God, let God be God, and learn to be just Mom.

It is a one moment at a time process, staying mindful about my crazy thinking, and turning toward a healthier letting go. I have to be curious about my emotional, cognitive, and spiritual state so I can consciously do what is healthy and loving for my parenting.

Now…years later, I walk beside him. He is navigating his life – sometimes beautifully and sometimes with starts and stops like the rest of us bozos on the bus - with the help of some amazing guides who are not named Mom. My letting go combined with having clearly marked guardrails has created a healthier openness in him toward me; I work daily on respecting his journey and trusting the process instead of micromanaging. He turns to me when he wants support and he asks specifically for what he wants. Sometimes I say "hell yes" and other times I say "no way." I say "hell yes" more.

What we want for our children is to grow in self-esteem and confidence because of themselves, not us. The same is true for those we lead at work: we want them to soar because of their strength and courage. Not ours.

As you can see, the seven strategies necessary to walk the way of life I call Connected Leadership start to weave together; it is hard to tell where one starts and another leaves off. Listening deeply contributes to curiosity. Curiosity encourages conscious connections. Empathy and curiosity are graceful dance partners.

As we continue to explore this way of life that builds Connected Leadership, we witness how, like with the universe, all things are interconnected and, as a result, why connection is a vital life force.

In a recent *Harvard Business Review* article, Warren Berger begins by writing, "When asked recently to name the one attribute CEOs will need most to succeed in the turbulent times ahead, Michael Dell, the chief executive of Dell, Inc., replied, 'I would place my bet on curiosity.'"[25]

Personally, I would double down on curiosity whenever given the chance.

Getting Curious about Curiosity: Mantras to Live a Curious Life

Over and over, research shows that curious people have a stronger sense of wellbeing.[26] Curiosity is an antidote to disconnection and disengagement. It expands our ability to tune in to others and improves our overall relational, social, and emotional health. These two reminders help strengthen the curiosity muscle.

Relish the new and stay open. People who try new things lead fuller lives. This means the very things we might shy away from could end up being an invitation to joy.

A few years ago, I tried something I wanted to do my whole life: skiing. I'd never been on a slope or worn skis. But I knew my time had come, especially since my son is a fearless and gifted skier.

I could not wait to get to the mountain. While I am not sure they can call what I was doing skiing, I was on skis and moving down a mountain in the Wasatch Mountains in Big Cottonwood Canyon in Utah. At the end of the day, as toddlers flew by me, skis pointed straight ahead, I reflected on why I had never skied up to this point in my life.

I grew up as a victim of "no." "No, you will get hurt." "No, we can't afford that." "No, it is too dangerous." "No, girls don't do that." As I recalled how I was taught that life is about saying "no," a man walked by and said to me, "I've been watching you. You're clearly the happiest person on this mountain today." My son thought that was creepy. I simply saw it as the universe sending a message: Keep saying "yes." Relish the new.

People grow before our eyes. We put people in a box by developing labels for them and their behavior. We send meta-messages and negative energy their way, reinforcing that how they once were is how they will always be. How different our interactions with people would be if we saw family members, colleagues, and friends, even the corner barista, as evolving creatures instead of someone to be changed or fixed—if we just accepted them and became curious about them; accepting people and not putting them in a box is different, however, from not having healthy discernment and boundaries. Some people and their behavioral patterns do not change, and we have to be mindful of that as previously mentioned.

Andy, an executive with whom I worked, had a specific way of looking at one of his colleagues, Michael. Andy's perspective was not wrong, but it was limited. Andy thought Michael was uncaring, self-centered, and somewhat arrogant. Much to Andy's surprise, when they were both working late one evening, Michael's sister dropped by the office with her baby. The way Michael interacted with his baby niece gave Andy a different perspective. After the sister and baby left, Andy said, "I never saw you with a kid before." Michael, who was young, single, and did not have children said, "I know. This baby grabbed my heart...kind of changed me." People grow before our eyes.

True curiosity is about living with a sense of openness. It is realizing that what we think we know can change at any minute through a conversation, an experience, or even an event that allows us to turn toward ourselves and others more honest, open, and willing.

Curious Conversations

Daniel Siegel, MD, is changing the way we think about the brain thanks to his groundbreaking work, the neurobiology of "we."[27] His studies suggest our relationships shape our neural architecture. How we are treated, communicated with, and regarded shape how we think about ourselves and respond to the world. Since communication is a key currency in the economy of relationships, we cannot overlook its importance in building connection.

Dr. Siegel's work helps scientifically corroborate what many of us intuitively know: the quality of our relationships and communications impacts not just who we are and how we react, but also the structure of our brains by programming us in certain ways based on the history of our interactions. Our neural pathways are formed by how we interpret, adjust to, and habitualize the relational patterns that occur around us. Those neural pathways then dictate our cognitive and behavioral patterns which can sometimes have less to do with what is currently happening and more about how our brains are wired based on our histories.

The good news: neuroplasticity means our brains can reorganize as we learn new skills, adopt new habits, or interact with people whose treatment of us lifts us up. As we work our brain differently, we develop a different repertoire of responses. Neuroplasticity inspires hope, because as we apply the practices that build connection, our brains are rewiring.

There is no such thing as an inconsequential communication. Since communication has the potential to lift us up or tear us down, then we must pick our words carefully and the people with whom we interact judiciously. Too often, the impact of words is overlooked and denied as people are called "too sensitive" or are told to develop a tougher skin. A single snarky word or a phrase meant to humiliate can shrivel a child's spirit, build walls in marriages, and demoralize a valued employee. Remember the school playground rhyme, "Sticks and stones may break my bones, but words will never hurt me"? Simply not true.

I have seen executives who earn seven figures become emotionally depleted because of the onslaught of consistent verbal attacks. I have seen teens shrink because of peers', teachers', or family members' verbal abuse. I have seen corporate team members go for cover and disengage while their leader consistently criticizes them. I have witnessed the demise of what once were loving relationships because of words: nasty, abusive, threatening, and shaming.

The challenge is to use words to build others up, to ensure our words match our actions, and to do so amidst the obstacles life throws in our paths. To do so as we struggle with financial demands as our spouse decides not to work. To do so as we tuck in a child who has trouble sleeping when we, ourselves, are exhausted. To do so as we face a colleague who has been fired as a result of behavioral struggles.

The following tips are designed to use curiosity as a relationship builder that first starts by strengthening the relationship with self before turning to others:

1. Prepare yourself before a conversation. This preparation means that you are asking yourself questions before having an important conversation:
   a. **What do I know for sure?** This is where you look at what you really know, not what you think you know.
   b. Then hit the pause button and ask: **What story am I telling myself?** This is where you use curiosity to understand what you are telling yourself to be true. Sometimes we tell ourselves stories to protect ourselves, blame the other person, stay stuck in old patterns, or just resist changing.
   c. **How do I want this to end?** This is where you use curiosity to be honest about the outcome you want.
2. The second group of questions focus on learning more about the other person and help you seek a deeper understanding:
   a. **What do I need/want to know about the other person or people involved?**
   b. **This focuses on asking questions that help you seek to understand: What is their perspective? How are they feeling?**
3. The third question in the preparation stage: **What more do I need to learn and understand about myself?**

   This is the bee's knees of curiosity questions because it is so connected to everything else. Our ability to lead, inspire, connect with, and engage others is deeply impacted by our ability to know ourselves. So here are some general questions to sit with before, during, and after a conversation:
   a. What gets brought up for me? What's underneath these feelings and my response?
   b. What historical experiences are being triggered for me, if any?
   c. What part have I played in getting us to this point?
   d. What part do I want to play in creating a different outcome?

Let me use an example from my own life to illustrate how one might go about employing these tips. One weekend morning, my husband, Greg, and I made plans to meet for lunch after he played racquetball. He was going to call me when he was finished, and we would choose a restaurant at that time. After our meal, he would then go to his office because it was tax season and as a CPA that meant he was just a little busy.

Greg called as he said he would. Sounding frustrated, he told me he had to go directly to the office and that his office manager would order in lunch for him and me. I was disappointed, but I reluctantly agreed, sounded a bit put out, and hung up.

I remember feeling crabby because of the change of plans; I did not want to have a rushed lunch in his office. So using the steps just illustrated, let's walk through the scenario again.

> *What do I know for sure?* What I knew for sure: I was looking forward to having lunch with my husband at a restaurant so we could relax and connect; he had to change the plans because of work demands.

> *What story am I telling myself?* The story I was telling myself went like this, "He must think I don't have anything else to do but change my plans to suit him." I was focusing on a negative interpretation that came from my own thinking and experiences; it really did not have anything to do with the situation.

> *How do I want this to end?* If I'm being honest, I would first say, "I don't care if I ever have lunch with him again; that's how I want this to end." But, if I allow myself to get curious and vulnerable, underneath that self-protective one-two punch is the truth. What I really wanted was this: to connect. I wanted to spend time with my husband. I also wanted him to understand that I am willing to be flexible in some situations. And I want wanted myself to understand that I don't have to say "yes" if a plan does not work for me. So, in summary, how I

really wanted this to end includes: me stopping my desire to please people, understanding that "no" is a complete sentence, and finding ways to deeply connect.

Once I was clear about the answers to the self-curiosity questions, I was ready to be curious about Greg.

What do I need/want to know about the other person? After hitting the pause button, which allowed me to breathe and get curious, I called Greg back. I was then able to say to him, "I'm just curious, honey. You're not the kind of person who typically changes plans at the last minute. What's going on?" He could tell the difference in my tone, so he felt more comfortable telling me a client had contacted him with an urgent request, and he simply needed to get to the office pronto.

What more do I need to learn and understand about myself? What gets brought up for me from my past? What part do I play in getting us to this point? What part do I want to play in creating a different outcome? I had been triggered in a nanosecond, because I had felt disregarded and unimportant. I have felt this way many times before, going back to my childhood. I felt overlooked when my mom was terminally ill and no one was keyed in to my feelings. The adults expected me to be understanding, helpful, and flexible at all times. By the age of ten, I was a world-class-fixer-and-denial-champion.

Creating a different outcome would go something like this: "Honey, I know I sounded crabby when you called about changing the lunch plans. I was. I was looking forward to having lunch the way we planned it. I know what came up was something you couldn't control. I wished I had just said that doesn't work for me and that I'll look forward to seeing you later when you come home. Instead, I shut down initially until I had time to process what was really going on with me."

It takes a tremendous amount of energy, time, and reeducation to slow down the process and our lightning-quick reactions. To be curious about why we react the way we do. As a reward for all of the effort, we can experience a deeper appreciation for ourselves and the impact our experiences have had on us. This allows us to change the dance steps and invite others into the same process.

Curiosity for Everyday Leading and Living

Because curiosity can strengthen our self-awareness and self-compassion, it also enhances the trust we have in ourselves. As a result, we do not need to practice the old patterns of disconnection that created harm, nor do we have to participate in the patterns of disconnection that others foist on us. And we most certainly do not need to participate in patterns that our curiosity teaches us are no longer creating the kind of connections that help us to thrive. We can be honest about what we need, even if someone tells us "no." We can risk, be curious, and set boundaries, because we can now create emotional safety for ourselves and others.

Many times, the emotionally safe places leaders create are positively influenced by the words, tone, and approach they choose. Some words and phrases—like these—create an environment of openness and safety.

- "I trust your judgment. Tell me what you're thinking."
- "What feels comfortable for you?"
- "I would love to know more about how you're feeling."
- "That sounds really tough (or another adjective based on what the person is describing)."
- "I don't have an answer. What do you think?"
- "Tell me more."
- "I know you can figure this out."
- "What do you think you could do that would be helpful?"
- "When you get in touch with your gut, what does it say?"

Our behavior and attitude can further enhance or take away from creating an emotionally safe place. It is very disconcerting when someone says, "Tell me more" while looking at their phone and/or sounding crabby or tired. It hurts when someone says, "I'm listening" while they do not respond at all, look at the TV, or read a document.

Some behaviors—like these—when accompanying the words suggested above create even more of a psychologically safe environment:

- Making eye contact
- Putting away all distractions
- Not multitasking but focusing on the conversation at hand
- Making sure that there is no eye-rolling, smirking, grimacing
- Letting someone finish what they are saying
- Giving a heads up if you need to take a break and being clear about when you will return to finish the conversation

As you reach out with curiosity and give the message you are present, your employee or family member, friend or manager then feels trusted, empowered, and prepared to navigate their emotions and the situation with confidence. Curiosity creates a safe emotional space in which the other person feels they can be confused, stressed, discouraged, sad, or whatever they are feeling without being concerned that you are losing faith in them or their work.

What follows are phrases that shut down curiosity and connection because they make others feel cross-examined or lectured, which leaves them feeling anxious and defensive:

- "How come?"
- "What were you thinking?"
- "Let me tell you how it is…."
- "Why?"
- "Didn't you realize?"
- "You need to…."
- "You always…."
- "You never…."

- "You should…."
- "As I said before…."
- "Whatever…."
- "At least…."
- "Once again…."

These litigator/auditor tactics, as I call them, oftentimes create unintentional outcomes in families and workplaces.

In the workplace, these dynamics happen when managers believe that "not knowing" is a sure sign of incompetence. As a result, and to be seen as the one who has a bright career ahead of them, employees puff up their own authority and walk around silverback-style, pounding their chests, fueling cultures of competition and comparison. They interrogate others, avoid having direct conversations, and resort to micromanaging, punishing, or shaming people. All this does is fortify disconnection and disengagement, the same way it does in families.

These approaches are common among parents who think they are the ones with the answers and who, as a result, try to manage their child's every emotion, response, and move. Rooted in the philosophy that parents truly know better, this is a prevalent and often damaging parenting trend these days. This fear-based philosophy reaffirms the mistaken belief that to raise law-abiding, content, and productive kids, the parents must treat the kids as if they are a project to be managed or a product to be marketed. This kind of parenting teaches children that they do not have the inner strength or healthy coping skills to navigate life and live from a place of authentic self.

This harmful dynamic also occurs in relationships between adults. Rather than putting things aside and truly listening to the emotions of another, adults immediately go into fix-it mode with other adults. Instead of finding ways to attune to and support another, solutions are pushed or questions are asked that shut down connection.

In summary, developing curiosity to deepen Connected Leadership in all parts of life means that:

- We ask curious questions that are empowering and open-ended.
- Our facial expressions and voice tones should invite openness.
- We show interest by asking questions that allow for a deeper understanding.
- We pace ourselves, asking one question at a time and giving the other person plenty of time to answer.
- We practice W.A.I.T. (Why Am I Talking?) and T.H.I.N.K (is what I am saying Thoughtful, Honest, Inspiring, Necessary, and Kind?)
- We use the power of the pause to create a sense of curiosity. Silence is healthy.

And yes, people open up when they are in the presence of connection-based curiosity. Employees become more empowered and motivated. Our children feel safer to be who they truly are. Marriages more intimate.

As we build the foundation to become a Connected Leader, we learn that leadership is less about a formula and more about owning and telling our story to enhance self-discovery, demonstrate curiosity in others, and inspire people to want the connection they see in us and our lives.

Connection Reflection: Celebrates Curiosity

o   As with all of the connection strategies, start first with
    yourself. How can you show yourself loving curiosity?
    Treat yourself as you would a sweet friend about whom
    you want to know more. Explore your own life and feel-
    ings with a trusted guide like a coach therapist, sponsor,
    or spiritual director.

o   Maintain a journal in which you ask yourself ques-
    tions to get to know yourself better, such as, "What
    have been important events in my life, and what impact
    did they have on me emotionally, spiritually, relation-
    ally?" "What brings me joy?" "How can I build more
    self-loving approaches into my life so I give myself the
    VIP treatment emotionally and spiritually?"

o   When you are speaking with others—whether they be
    your board, your executive team, your employees, your
    spouse, or your children—try to weave in the super-
    power of all responses: "Tell me more." It helps them
    to open up.

o   Find ways to step into the "sacred awe" Einstein referred
    to. How can you be in awe of all that happens in life?
    How can you search for the miraculous and sacred,
    the meaningful and interconnected? How can you de-
    velop ways to find the God of your understanding more
    consistently?

Chapter Six

Demonstrates Accountability:
Closing the Escape Hatches

"Wisdom stems from personal accountability. We all make mistakes; own them... learn from them. Don't throw away the lesson by blaming others."

—Steve Maraboli

Lessons from a Place of Humility

Alex, the managing partner of a boutique consulting firm, asked for my help immediately after I had met with him and his team. He wanted to discuss what I had been teaching: how our normalized negative behaviors can tear people down. He said he felt stunned, because that same morning, his college-aged daughter had told him, "Dad, you tear others down. You've spent your life building yourself up, bullying us, and proving you are right."

As he participated in the discussion I had with his team, he felt a small stab of concern that maybe his daughter had raised some points worth considering. "I didn't give it too much thought until you started to talk about the same thing: how we can be self-righteous, judge others, blame, and shame because we feel it's easier than examining ourselves."

He went on to tell me that he had come home the previous week to find his wife was filing for divorce. She was done with the stress his behavior caused the entire family. They had been in therapy a few times, but it was difficult, he recalled, for him to take it seriously, own his mistakes, and to make working on himself a priority. He was genuinely beside himself as he thought of life without her. In spite of all of his hurtful behavior, he loved her but did not know how to show it other than by providing financial comforts and focusing on details like getting the car fixed and asking about household repairs.

He said, "Between my daughter's comments, my wife filing for divorce, and my human resources executive telling me that a hostile work environment complaint was filed against me, I am overwhelmed. It feels like God is using a megaphone to get my attention." This was undoubtedly the universe's version of a supersized message.

I knew, based on experience, that these dark moments of the soul can invite us to commit to the hard work required to change. So together, Alex and I laid out what my work with him would entail. If he was going to be a Connected Leader at work and home, he was signing up for the ride of his life. Since there is no outside solution to an inside problem, he was going to have to speak truth to the misdirected, unhealthy power of his own ego and learn to demonstrate accountability.

What Is Accountability?

Accountability means that the ugly, irresponsible, mean stuff we say and do happens on our watch. It means the escape hatches close. We become open to the lessons hidden in our mistakes, and we don't back away. We acknowledge and accept that what we have done or said has sometimes harmed others and ourselves. We admit the lies we tell ourselves to justify our fear-based responses keep us stuck. We commit to changing what we need to change and find ways to make amends to others when it is wise to do so.

What I know is this: accountability is difficult to embrace, because it means we can no longer lean on the excuses. What is life without excuses? Damn hard. This is why:

- Gone are the days we can blame losing our temper on our teenager's demanding behavior.
- Gone are the days we justify our gossiping about others instead of admitting that we feel wounded and scared.
- Gone are the days we explain away our road rage, our emotional ugliness, or our drama-creating people-berating by saying "they" are the problem.

Before you decide you want to live a life of accountability, understand this: if you undertake this connection strategy, it gets more difficult to take the detours you were used to taking down the roads of indirect communication, under-the-breath mutterings, and grudge-holding. Those roads are closed if you are going to choose accountability over blame (making someone else responsible for our choices and behaviors) and shame (feeling as if you are unworthy and wanting to dump the same feeling on someone else).

Before you decide to live a life of accountability, recognize that you will be embarking on an emotional archeological dig. This journey will uncover the layers of life experiences that contribute to your behavioral, emotional, and cognitive processes today. Underneath the blame, for instance, might be fear and self-loathing. Underneath the gossip, as an example, is the need to pump yourself up.

First, we step into accountability by being gentle with ourselves. This means that we accept our missteps, learn how to be self-compassionate, and embrace the lessons we are open to learning.

Second, we value accountability because it builds trust. As we trust ourselves more, we hold others more accountable as well—not through scolding words and haphazard consequences, but through empathy and loving boundaries. As we take ownership for our lives and choices, how we show up and how we shut down, others feel safer with us and believe we are more trustworthy because—simply put—we are.

If stillness rocks and curiosity empowers, then accountability frees, because not being honest about our behaviors and who we are keeps us locked in our secrets, shame, and blame. Accountability releases us from this isolation.

As with most things in this book, it might sound easy. But, also as with most things in this book, it isn't. The thing about being accountable is once you commit to it, it is almost impossible to sidestep it. You might want to go back in time to the days that you lied to yourself about your motives or found a way to shirk responsibility or validated your behavior, but it is hard to go back to sleep once you have awakened. And in time, you realize that a life of connecting consciously, listening deeply, celebrating curiosity, exhibiting empathy, and demonstrating accountability is cleaner and freer.

Being accountable leaves you marveling at how much healthier your relationships are while also realizing how much is required of you in courageously emotional ways. There is no turning back to a world of emotional disconnection once you taste what it is like to strengthen relationships because you are accountable.

The Fearful Self and Accountable Self

To be accountable, we have to release ourselves from the stronghold of fear.

Fear is a neurobiological response triggered in the amygdala, and it stems from our primitive fight-or-flight response. Although we are no longer running from the saber-toothed tiger, we are still running from fears related to rejection, unworthiness, criticism, and abandonment. Fear can help us know when we feel emotionally or physically threatened. It protects us when warranted. It also can lead us to feel we might be endangered even if we are not; these are the times we are invited to go deeper into ourselves in order to heal ourselves from lingering, emotional wounds that trip us up.

How can we understand the protective, bona fide power of fear? How can we also acknowledge the damage it does when it hijacks us emotionally and causes us to lash out and hurt people who are not responsible for the historical wounds we still harbor?

Fear can become a way of life. We all have a fearful self, developed from our experiences with loss, powerlessness, scarcity, anxiety, and trauma. Fear forms a stronghold within the heart, soul, and brain that primes us to expect rejection and anticipate humiliation. We fear that we will not get the job, the romantic interest, the raise, or the college admission. We fear we will not be a good parent. Good spouse. College-bound athlete. We live in a boiling pot of fears and anxieties that can unconsciously push us into emotional reactions that become habitual, woven into the fabric of our personalities and the neural pathways of our brains.

Alex, who we met earlier in this chapter, quickly learned his fear catapulted him into abusive verbal responses: he lashed out, humiliated, scorned, and controlled. His impact was heartbreaking—traumatic to others and destructive to him.

Raised in a rigid family, Alex's curiosity was extinguished at an early age and replaced by a dutiful compliance that earned him favor from those in charge. Feelings were not attuned to. Questions not celebrated. Basically, he had no time to connect consciously, listen deeply, and celebrate curiosity. He was not encouraged to figure out who he truly was, how he was feeling, and what he believed. His dutiful compliance helped him succeed in school, at church, and on the basketball court; but it also encouraged him to hide his sense of inadequacy behind a wall of self-righteousness. His emotions scared him, so he belittled others for theirs. He feared he was going to make a mistake, so he focused on creating a perfect, no-fault-found-with-me life. He developed dysfunctional and addictive habits to help him deal with his deep-seated fears of being devalued, misunderstood, and rejected. Alex, in this way, was no different than the rest of us clowns, stumbling through life: struggling with unresolved hurts that gain strength with each passing, unconscious day.

Like Alex, many of us live in fear, even though we might have all the outer trappings of success. While the car we drive, the job we have, the house we live in, and the posts we create may signal to the outside world that we are okay, our emotional landscape can be littered with landmines. Until we connect intentionally, listen deeply, and get curious about ourselves with a healthy dose of self-empathy, we continue to participate in cognitive patterns and interpersonal behaviors that prevent us from having the relationships we desire with ourselves and others.

It gets even nuttier. By stepping away from accountability, we keep the unhealthy patterns alive. "None of this could possibly be my fault," we tell ourselves. We become mired in denial and hone our ability to tell ourselves stories that let us off the hook when we need to be on it. We tell ourselves tales that reinforce our holier-than-thou, defensive, angry, judgmental, and anxious behaviors. These stories justify how we blame, criticize, and scapegoat others. These stories are a result of unhealed insecurities.

And while many moons ago someone who had power over us treated us meanly or abused us, that day is long gone and yet, we live as if it is not. This is how unresolved trauma works, and even sometimes works after we are consciously awakening and healing. Trauma wires us to believe that we will be hurt again or betrayed or abused. It sets us up to have reactions and make choices that undermine who we are truly. Even when the threat is no longer around or even alive, we can respond from a place of fear and shame. It keeps us responding in unhealthy ways, damaging ourselves, and hurting others who are not traumatizing us. Unpacking this with trusted healers who can help us understand how to keep ourselves safe, grounded in the present, and leaning into the tools of healthy connection is critical.

The moment we begin to soften our fear-based responses toward ourselves is the moment we begin to soften toward others. The moment we begin to simply observe our intense feelings instead of acting on them is the moment we begin to choose our response. The moment we begin to accept the feelings we believe are unacceptable is the moment we begin to accept others.

Two practices are key to being a connected, accountable leader: *making amends* and *creating boundaries*. And neither of these healing practices can be performed alone: we learn how to do these in community with others who are also committed to the same journey of wellbeing and healing.

Let's look at what I mean by making amends and creating boundaries in greater detail.

Accountability and Making Amends

It takes a great deal of humility and vulnerability to accept that we have done or said something hurtful. It is hard. We look furtively around for the escape hatches. Yet, we realize that taking the escape hatches of blame, shame, denial, and other not-so-healthy responses will only take us back to a place that did not work for us originally, try as we may to validate our escape. So now what? Now that we have given up those ever-so-welcoming, seductive excuses, what do we replace them with?

Making amends is more than saying, "I'm sorry." Sometimes, a person will apologize when they are simply going through the motions of the culturally acceptable, polite thing to do, even though they don't have a clue about how hurtful their behavior was. We have all given an apology like this. We have all received an apology like this. Believe me, it is not worth the words.

Here are the steps to a real apology, through which we focus on making amends for the wrongdoing, big or small:

- **Apologize by showing sincerity in the words, tone, and energy you give off.** Your apology should demonstrate that you spent time and effort reflecting on what you did that was harmful. Use the words "I apologize for...." Finish the sentence with specifics about what you said and/or did. For example: "I apologize for stepping out of my lane and lashing out at you." "I apologize for lying." "I apologize for being late and not calling." "I apologize for missing the deadline and not giving you a heads up."

- **Acknowledge your feelings about the harm you did. State the impact you believe your behavior had on the other person; combine this with curiosity.** Use words like, "I feel sad because I believe I hurt you when I lied about you. And I would like it if you could tell me more how my behavior impacted you." Or "I feel disappointed in myself. I know I let you down when I missed the deadline. And I would appreciate it if you could tell me what that felt like for you."

  If they are willing to tell you, just say, "Thank you for telling me that" when they are finished. Do not defend, explain, or talk anymore about what they or you did.

- **Ask if they can accept your apology and forgive you**; remember their forgiving you is for them, not for you. It is not their job to help you feel better. It is their job to free themselves from resentment for their own wellbeing, and it is your job to humble yourself in the hopes that you don't keep repeating the same hurtful patterns.

- **Tell them what you are doing to change your behavior and invite them to give you feedback.** The most effective apology is not verbal; it is behavioral. A verbal apology without behavioral change is just a manipulation.

  We can all use nice-sounding words to get what we want without being genuinely sorry, accountable, or willing to change our emotional and behavioral patterns. To change our behavior, we must add supportive routines and structures to our lives to help us transform. As an example, "I have decided to get into therapy to explore why I make up stories about others." "I am going to talk to my mentor about time management techniques." "I am going to talk to my sponsor about this pattern and really get honest."

Something needs to change if we want to change the impact we have on others and our own lives.

- **Thank them again for giving you the opportunity to apologize.** This sounds something like this, "Thank you for hearing me out and giving me a chance to apologize." You can also invite ongoing feedback from those who truly have your back: "I hope you're willing to point out examples if you see me doing this again."

- **Make amends.** This is what you do to change the behavior. No apology is as powerful as changing a behavior. Again, a verbal apology without behavioral change is just manipulation.

Alex decided he first had to apologize to his family. He wanted to apologize, because it was the courageous and healthy thing to do. This meant he had to let go of control over the outcome. He had to believe that he was apologizing not to get back in people's good graces, but because it was the way to clean up the mess he consistently created. That night at home, he asked if he could speak to his three children and his wife, who was still focused on going through with the divorce. No one really wanted to hear what he had to say. But they gathered anyway, just to get it over with.

Alex was ready.

"I am sorry for all the hurt I have caused over the years. I have criticized, humiliated, and bullied you with my words. I have lashed out and raged. My behavior embarrassed you and shut you down. Instead of understanding your perspective and your feelings, I lectured. Instead of being a loving husband and supportive father, I was belittling. Whenever you are willing to tell me, in detail, about how I've hurt you, I'll be ready to listen. If you're not willing to talk to me, I understand, because I certainly have not made it emotionally safe to be open with me in the past. What needs to change is me. I have failed you. These are just words until you see my changed behaviors. I know that. So, I plan on living every day differently, and I hope you feel and see the difference so you can forgive me."

Alex continued to be coached, along with his team, at work. He agreed to see a therapist with his wife, who was now reconsidering the divorce based on the consistent changes she observed over significant time. Alex started a more regular exercise program. He got up early to meditate. He spent time with each of his children, checking in with them every day. They got used to hearing him say, "Please tell me what today was like for you." He kept at it, even if they, understandably, blew him off. When his family talked, he listened. No running in with a solution. No advice giving. No criticism or comparison. Just tuning into their feelings and providing a safe container.

Every day, Alex woke up and prayed he would find the strength to treat everyone, including himself, with kindness and compassion. He would find himself often saying the "Serenity Prayer" quickly during times of stress, when historically he would have lashed out: "God grant me the serenity to accept the things I cannot change, courage to change the things I can, and wisdom to know the difference." He found that the power of the words grounded him and put the focus where it needed to be: on changing himself.

He made a similar apology to his team members at work. They were initially just as dumbfounded as his family. But they slowly saw the consistent actions behind the words—nothing happened overnight. It was not a flipping of the switch. It was consistent differences over many, many months that got people to trust that maybe the changes were sticking.

Eventually, the work atmosphere became more enjoyable, more productive. They were able to grow the business and look at disappointments as opportunities to learn. They stopped having so many resignations. They had more talented people apply for employment. And two years after Alex started his odyssey of accountability and self-discovery, his firm won "Best Place to Work" in their city.

His family were there to see him accept his award. He told his story during his acceptance speech: how he had lived a life of inner turmoil despite outside success, and how he had treated harshly those who worked for him and those whom he loved. He told the story about his epiphany, and he thanked his team for giving him another chance to be a Connected Leader and his family for walking beside him on the journey of deeper connections.

It was a powerful evening. As Alex wrapped up his acceptance speech, his last sentence was this: "Once I learned to step in and be accountable, I learned real freedom. Genuinely apologizing takes a relationship to a new level, because it breathes connection into conflict, hurt, and confusion."

Accountability and Creating Boundaries

Leaders who are accountable are willing and open to changing their behavior. As a result, other people's batshit-crazy behavior is no longer acceptable, either.

I remember driving our then-seven-year-old son home from school one day. Even at that very early age, he was the accountability barometer in our family, yet with all the innocence of a child. I was complaining about something or someone. I'm sure it was annoying, as I could not have been very inspiring to be around. He quietly turned to me and without batting an eye said, "Stop." Well, that about sums it up.

Years later, when I was nagging him about some comments his social media followers made that had nothing to do with him but were crass and ugly, he looked at me with the same clarity of thought he had had ten years earlier, but this time with more maturity: "If you continue to obsess about this, you will drive yourself insane. I have done nothing wrong so please stop putting your fears on me."

If that story does not resonate with you, then how about this one? A CEO gathered his team, to include all of his direct reports, for a brief meeting because he was tired about some organizational issues and wanted a change. It lasted less than a minute. When everyone was assembled, he simply said:

> We have created a culture of gossip and sabotage. I have contributed to it. Mostly everyone does. It stops.

Now. I have set the wrong tone. It is bad for us and bad for business. Starting tomorrow, we, as an executive team, will be receiving coaching on how to be trustworthy, connected, emotionally healthy, world-class empowering executives. We will work together as a collective group, and we will all do our own individual work too. I understand it is the best investment we can make. It's best we just leave it at that for now until we can receive the expertise we need to treat ourselves and each other better.

Think about how much safer and more productive environments are when we are directly communicating in healthy ways. Think about the possibility inherent in compassionately giving feedback to others, instead of being huddled around the water cooler talking about someone for entertainment's sake or lashing out at them in judgmental ways. Think about the healing that can take place in a family when everyone's part in the family drama is acknowledged, instead of scapegoating one person for being "the" problem.

When we practice self-accountability and ask others to be accountable, we are practicing brave and loving compassion. It is brave because not everyone wants to be held accountable. It is courageous because respectfully and directly offering feedback is harder and requires more vulnerability than gossiping.

Some people will turn away from the feedback, trash the boundary, and use your directness as more fuel for their fire of shame and blame. Not everyone is ready to take the invitation to live a life of connection and accountability. Some will never take it.

For years I put up with a situation I knew was toxic, but one I was sure I could turn around. The actual details do not really matter. What is more important is, as I said before in this book, what we learn about ourselves and how we commit to growth, transformation, and awakening when we go through situations designed to teach us.

Most of us have situations that we put up with for a variety of reasons; in this scenario, I thought I was putting up with the poor treatment I was receiving for reasons I thought admirable. However, the reasons were really a part of my self-sabotaging thinking. I wanted to be a positive influence and thought I could change others through my consistent thoughtful, generous, and accepting ways. However, it was another example of my hustling for approval, thinking that if I could change some pretty wounded behavior in others I would prove myself worthy, loveable, and able—single-handedly—to be the reason someone else was saved.

Eventually, I looked at myself in the mirror, had a moment of sanity, and said, "No more." I had been spending my energy feeding sugar cubes to the bear, and the only result was I was worn down, and therefore, more vulnerable to the bear.

I surrendered (I am a frequent visitor in the land of surrendering, folks). By putting up with the situation and complaining about it, my behavior was the only problem that needed my attention. I changed what I could change; I stopped trying to tell people—who did not care—how their treatment of me was painful. I refrained from being an emotional pit stop for people racing through to fill their tanks with my precious fuel. It was hard and not just a little unnerving to make this change, and I needed help from my cheering squad on a daily basis.

As I made this change and had all kinds of self-doubts doing so, I spent months practicing self-compassion with the help of therapists and healthy people who pointed out I had been attending a three-ring circus not of my making. I learned to stop attending. It was scary. It was healing. It was a relief to no longer deal with those crazy monkeys and a barking ringmaster.

I chose long periods of solitude, listening deeply to the divine words of healing. I put down my lifelong pursuit of approval mostly aimed toward those who were going to forever reject me anyway, regardless of who I was. And I realized that the unconscious questions looping in my heart and soul could be put to rest if I recognized and lovingly held them: "Am I good enough? Am I loveable even though I could not save my mother?"

Quite frankly, I got to the point where I learned this truth; we cannot simultaneously be our best selves and avoid pissing off people. When we align our actions with the divine, good, orderly direction we seek, some folks will not like that we are changing the dance steps. There are more people having hissy fits in response to boundaries than child-stars in rehab; people typically do not like boundaries. Especially those who were benefitting from our lack of self-respect.

Keep these few steps and tips in mind when setting boundaries:

- We set a boundary for ourselves to stay emotionally, physically, and/or spiritually safe. The boundary is not for the other person and it is not a punishment; they are not going to send you a potted plant as a "thank you for the boundary" present. Really, they are not. We no longer need the protection of anger and rage anymore, because we have a more potent protection: we have our connected, accountable, curious, self-respecting, empathetic, mindful trustworthy self.
- Setting a boundary can also invite growth in the other and a deeper connection. How they respond is a clear indication of where they are; pay attention.
- Setting boundaries allows us to treasure our hearts and gifts; it is a spiritual principle grounded in all the ancient spiritual teachings and texts.

This is what boundaries can sound like:

- **To a family member:** I'm uncomfortable with you talking about me behind my back. I'm happy to talk with you about it, but not until you stop doing this. Let me know what you are willing to do to change and until you do I'm going to limit my interactions with you.
- **To a boss:** I felt disappointed when I was not asked to attend the pitch after I worked so hard on it. I would like to attend the next meeting with you and hope you will consider that. I have a request for the future: Next time could you please share

with me, in advance, what role you see me playing so we are on the same page?

- **To a four-year-old:** I feel sad you hit your brother. I'm going to ask you to sit in this chair until you can calmly tell me what happened. Then I want you to apologize to your brother and do something kind for him.

- **To a teenager:** It's not okay when you miss curfew. I feel concerned and worried because I'm thinking of all the dangerous things that could happen. We're building trust here and I hope you understand how I feel. Because you broke curfew, you will not be able to go out for the rest of the weekend; we ask you to find some way to repair the trust. Honoring our family guidelines is a way of life for us.

- **To a colleague:** I'm angry because I worked all weekend to deliver that project on time after you did not do what you said you would do. I feel taken advantage of. I want you to know that unless we can find a more collaborative way of working, I'm hesitant to work with you again.

- **To an employee:** On numerous occasions, we have talked about how you can come across as dismissive. So here is what we will do: we will provide you with a coach. We support you and want you to change this behavior. If you don't want to work with the coach, or if after nine months of working with the coach we don't see a consistent change, we will visit other options.

- **To a significant other:** It scares me when you get angry at the other drivers on the road because I feel this puts our family in danger, and I worry about what our kids are learning about anger. If this doesn't change, I would prefer we take separate cars, and then we can enjoy each other when we arrive at our destination.

- **To a parent:** When you yell at me, I shut down. I feel embarrassed, rejected, and scared. Next time you yell, I'm going to take some space until you calm down and then we can talk.

We can heal shame and transform the worlds we occupy by bringing a mindfulness to all interactions, by sharing our vulnerabilities, opening up about our mistakes, and changing what we can change.

Much like the Japanese practice of *kintsugi*, in which broken pieces of china and pottery are glued back together with liquid gold, our cracks and imperfections need to be highlighted, not hidden. We learn to celebrate the broken places in ourselves by being accountable. And we learn how and where and with whom to share those cracks.

We are all broken in our own ways, but the brokenness morphs into a beautiful strength when we accept our wrongdoings, are willing to learn and step away from the flaws that keep us stuck, do what we need to do to align our hearts and brains in healthy ways, and commit to being in relationships with others who are strengthening their emotional and spiritual wholeness.

Connection Reflection: Demonstrates Accountability

o   Start owning your own stuff. All accountability starts with the self. Find accountability partners who can help you take responsibility for your behavioral and emotional patterns and who support you putting down the burdens you are carrying.

o   Develop daily ways to reflect honestly on what you have done, what you have left undone, and what you wish you had done differently. Celebrate the times you show up in connected, healthy ways. Remind yourself to act differently when you make missteps. Have at least one ride-or-die buddy with whom you can share your struggles as you learn to close the escape hatches.

o   Practice the apology steps outlined in this chapter: at home and at work.

Chapter Seven

Navigates Chaos Comfortably: The Gifts and Lessons

"All great changes are preceded by chaos."
—Deepak Chopra

My cellphone rang as our house was winding down and turning in for the night. I answered the call from one of my clients and quickly learned that he was not calling to discuss his upcoming presentation to the board, for which he had been preparing for weeks. Rather, he was calling to tell me they had rushed his daughter to the hospital with a drug overdose.

For months, we had discussed his heartache watching her addiction. Now, with the crisis at a crescendo, the importance of the presentation faded. Untethered and overwhelmed by life, the family dropped everything to deal with their tsunami of grief and fear.

My client is the typical captain of industry—he wanted to control, fix, rescue, and find the solution. He wanted to crawl into a cave when he realized his typical mode of problem-solving could not save his daughter. He chose another option: a path of surrender, acceptance, presence. He accepted his own emotional free-falling and kept the vigil with her. His commitment to his own emotional and spiritual wellbeing during this terrifying time, along with his ability to tune in to others, paved the way for his family to do the same.

Weeks later, after his daughter had entered treatment and the rest of the family was also receiving support, my client did present to the board. It was a grand slam, but that was not the thing of which he was the proudest. He was proudest of how he was beginning to show up everywhere he went: as a different man than he might have been if he had not endured such utter chaos. He showed up as a man who had fallen further than he ever thought he would under the burden of grief and fear. As a man who confronted wrenching heartbreak, stayed with it, and used it to deepen his connections to himself, to his purpose, and to others.

If we are honest about how messy our daily lives can be, we admit there is struggle, uncertainty, chaos, and change in every business setting, family scenario, and interpersonal relationship. Some days we are up to the challenge and move through uncertainty with confidence; on other days, one more thing pushes us over the edge. There might even be times that the ostrich mode sounds appealing: sticking our heads in the sand and pretending all is well. When I feel the all-too-familiar feeling of overwhelm flow over me, my first response is to stop what I am doing and find some way to pull the symbolic (or real) blanket over my head. I want to retreat, slip away, and forget.

But what I most likely do instead is call someone and talk it through. Connection is the antidote.

No matter the case, chaos occurs throughout life and leadership. So, with that said, Connected Leaders learn to embrace it and redirect its impact on their lives. Connected Leaders benefit from trusting that when their lives might feel like they are falling apart, they are, in fact, moving into place.

This surely does not feel good, but it holds good.

Chaos Is the New Normal

Chaos, in all its myriad forms, seeps into our lives. It shows up regardless of the elaborate routines and protective distractions we create. It slithers in despite our talents and hard work. Sometimes it comes when we least expect it; other times, we can feel its slow, steady approach.

Chaos and the ensuing painful feelings cannot be kept at bay simply because we have a demanding calendar, a board meeting to facilitate, a college degree to obtain, or a parent orientation to attend. When our son was younger, I used to say, "I am just one cough away"—his—"from calendar chaos"—mine. And now, while the same is not true any longer, the emotional response I feel, to any pain I believe I want to fix, can be the same.

There is no escaping chaos and suffering; it's part of the order of things. This does not mean that leaders like the unsettling events and accompanying difficult, sometimes heartbreaking, feelings at home, at work, or in the community.

It does mean that learning how to navigate the times of upheaval with a calm dignity and a turning inward is required to move through them. And while optimism and resilience are important components of navigating chaos with calm, we first must stay with the grief and uncomfortable feelings long enough to create a genuinely healthy optimism and resilience; we can't leapfrog over the tough stuff prematurely. We must stay present. Our ability to do so and accept the feelings with mindfulness, empathy, and curiosity is what builds authentic optimism and resilience, as opposed to dismissive, forced "positivity," which can be toxic.

Staying open to the whole experience is the job for leaders who want to deepen connection. Elizabeth Lesser beautifully captures this in her book *Broken Open*:

> "Adversity is a natural part of being human. It is the
> height of arrogance to prescribe a moral code or health
> regime or spiritual practice as an amulet to keep things

from falling apart. Things do fall apart. It is in their nature to do so. When we try to protect ourselves from the inevitability of change, we are not listening to the soul. We are listening to our fear of life and death, our lack of faith, our smaller ego's will to prevail. To listen to your soul is to stop fighting with life—to stop fighting when things fall apart; when they don't go our away, when we get sick, when we are betrayed or mistreated or misunderstood. To listen to the soul is to slow down, to feel deeply, to see ourselves clearly, to surrender to discomfort and uncertainty and to wait."[28]

Chaos is shapeless, but it is not without impact. It leaves us feeling queasy, tired, angry, anxious, depressed, overwhelmed, and eager to gain back the control that we never had to begin with but for which we still yearn. We lose our footing when it hits. We feel deserted by ourselves, others, and perhaps even God. We are in an emotional freefall.

It is in this vortex of chaos that we can discover wisdom and possibility, by leaning into the reality of the situation including our feelings. Rosamund Stone Zander and Benjamin Zander write in their inspiring book, *The Art of Possibility*:

"The foremost challenge for leaders today, we suggest, is to maintain the clarity to stand confidently in the abundant universe of possibility, no matter how fierce the competition, no matter how stark the necessity to go for the short-term goal, no matter how fearful people are, and no matter how urgently the wolf may appear to howl at the door. It is to have the courage and persistence to distinguish the downward spiral from the radiant realm of possibility in the face of any challenge."[29]

The leaders I marvel at maintain clarity, contentment, and hope—while they accept the reality of all their feelings—regardless of how loud the wolf is howling; they accept the chaos and, in the process, find the path to wholeness in their personal lives and their professional careers, integrating the lessons learned.

The Gift of Chaos: Painting Beauty from the Ashes

Many of us work to avoid chaos and its first cousins, uncertainty and anxiety, at all costs. We likely all have an active infrastructure in place to ensure that our personal and professional lives flow in an orderly manner, resting in routines designed to enhance a sense of security, and fortifying the mechanisms we use to convince ourselves we are actually in control.

Yet no matter how often or how much we plan, chaos is simply a natural part of life. The hurricane rages. The disease rapidly progresses. The relationship sputters and ends. The child suffers. The texting driver rear-ends us. People behave in disappointing ways.

The goal is not to control the chaos, try as we might. The goal is not to ignore it, fight it, or resist it. The goal is to listen to its message, repurpose it, and accept it. All healthy connections and spirituality are about letting go, because it is in the letting go that we learn to be present, honoring our own story and letting others have their journey.

Last summer I took Matthew and two of his close buddies to Montana. We had an amazing trip, and one of the reasons why is because it was one big letting go for me. From sunup to sundown, I went with the flow. The boys did their thing. I did mine. We met up for meals and some activities. It was magic.

One day, the boys went cliff-jumping, twenty-five feet down into an icy pool of water: glacier-cold. It was breathtaking watching them embody such free-spirited joy. No fear. Sheer boyishness in all the most wonderful ways. And then Matthew asked me to join them on the cliff, and for the life of me, I have no idea why I moved my feet forward, through the river. As I passed by Mark and Brett, who joined us that day as our guides, Mark said to me, "When Matthew is faced with a situation he feels unsure about in the future, how do you want him to approach it and how are you going to model that for him today?" I heard his words, they registered, and all of a sudden my sense of purpose was ignited; I turned and went into full on warrior-momma-courageous-mode while being terrified, completely out of my comfort zone. Up the cliff I went. And on the ledge I found myself, staring down into the black, slowly-moving water. It was as if something else took over, because I am surely not a daredevil; I was raised by a mother who believed that riding our bikes in the driveway could be fatal.

With each encouraging chant from the boys to "jump, jump!" I became more resistant to jumping. I stepped to the edge several times, realized I could not even move let alone jump, backed away again tears burning in my eyes.

With every act of resistance, with every slow moving second, Matthew and his two buddies reignited their efforts to see this momma jump. I wanted to lay down on the ledge and cry. I found myself swearing at these three young men whom I love greatly telling them to, "Shut up!"—my language was a bit more colorful in real life. Our two guides were standing in the river below capturing it all on video, including my swearing.

I was not only afraid to jump. I was terrified that once I hit the icy cold water my body would seize up and I would die of a heart attack. All the horrible stories I had ever heard about people doing crazy things rushed through my head.

After about ten minutes of sheer terror with my physical body clamping onto the rocks and ledge as if my life depended on it, it all went quiet. The boys stopped yelling for me to jump, and all I heard was silence. Quietly, I said to Matthew who was standing right next to me, "I can't let go."

And quietly, in turn, he said, "You have let go. You have." He was right. And yet, letting go is not a one-and-done; every time we let go, the universe converges to encourage us to let go even more. It is not fair that this whole letting go process is never done but it is a rinse-repeat part of life.

And with that, I felt as if I was lifted up by a power greater than me because as with all letting go, I was not capable of releasing my death-grip by my own sheer will. I hit the water—one miracle. I came to the surface (breathing and not seizing up—another miracle) and headed toward the shore with our guide, Brett, reaching out to help if I needed it. Matthew said it was not pretty; but I did it. Just like life.

There was an outburst of sheer elation and celebration and whoops and hollers from the man-boys still on the cliff, and it was all caught on video for posterity. Brett said to me, "I knew you were going to jump when you said 'I can't let go.' I knew that was the moment."

And so it is with life when we are called to come to the edge and let go. We hang on and clutch tighter and then the invisible hands peel back our fingers once we emotionally signal—even with the slightest wink of surrender—that we are ready. When the moment of release occurs and we exhale into that sweet mercy, we become one of the ones then able to help others find their way through chaos and uncertainty, grief and fear.

Letting go is best done with a tribe of people cheering us on.

When it comes to leadership in the workplace, far too often executives do not know how to let go, and therefore they struggle with the moving pieces of chaos and the ensuing frustrations and uncertainties: how to execute a product recall; how to offer an organizational apology when an executive has abused an employee; how to deal with the human side of the reorganization equation; how to battle in the marketplace when threats seemingly lurk behind every corner; how to deal with a high-level executive who sabotages others.

In our personal lives, we also feel under siege with the moving pieces of chaos: how to navigate an upcoming retirement that will create huge shifts at home; how to help a younger child when an older sibling has the Midas touch; how to deal with the disruption of an extramarital affair; how to adjust to a quiet house when the last child leaves for college; how to stay calm in the midst of backbreaking debt; how to trust that the light will come again when darkness surrounds us.

The sooner we know we cannot make everything all better, the better and braver we will be. By venturing into vulnerability, we become intimately aware of who we are. We see things differently because we no longer fear being "found out." And this makes it so much easier to show up honestly, with humility, willingness and openness. As we make this choice, we eventually experience the resilience that comes from incorporating our failings and fears into our identity as whole yet flawed people, inspiring other whole yet flawed people.

Even though I know this works slowly and with time, I don't always do it. When I don't do it, I am thankful I have a circle of people around me to whom I can say, "I screwed up again." And they smile and nod and sometimes share their wisdom, because they, too, have their own version of the same, underlying desire: to control the chaos instead of learning how to breathe through it.

There is a relatively unknown goddess from Hindu mythology by the name of Akhilandeshvari, which means "never not broken." She symbolizes the brokenness that leads to greater strength; the brokenness that takes us out of our cozy lives and shakes us up so that we can find our purpose; the brokenness that creates a crack so the light pours in; the brokenness that takes an individual from hiding the shame-creating parts of their lives to choosing the kind of courageous honesty that releases us.

The day I was handing this book to my publisher for another round of edits, I had a breakdown of sorts—I had been writing and editing for days on end. I was aware of the privilege of writing and also what it extracts; I get to relish the writing life but not without it also bringing me to my knees.

A few hours before I would have to push the "send" button, I experienced one of those raw and real times, when a letting go brings up all the things we hang onto. I found myself walking around my house, in the same outfit I had worn for a couple of days, crying and reliving some painful moments in my life when I felt alone and tender, vulnerable and scraped down to the bone. Re-reading and editing the words I had painstakingly written in this book brought up many of the fears of endings and beginnings, releasings and surrenderings, unworthiness and unlovability.

I thought I would exhale a sign of relief when I was ready to hand this book back again to my editor, instead I was broken wide open. My son—on whom I took out not just a little of my grief—kept the vigil, not quite sure how to take the next moment, and my golden retriever was glued by my side, in full-codependent-mode frantic that my tears signaled some terrible irreparable cracking.

Brokenness can come when we least expect it. It is a steady companion along with awakening. My response to this most recent difficult experience was to call a gifted therapist and spiritual guide and say, "Do you have room for me? Now? I have to get back to doing some serious work...soon." Heaven help us, this work of connection and leadership, growth and grace is the work of a lifetime.

This brokenness—which heals us and teaches us what we need to lovingly accept about ourselves—feels like it is cracking us wide open in the moments, days, and even, in some cases, the years that it sets up permanent camp. But it is preparing us for greater strength and clarity if we can accept that we are "never *not* broken," yet whole in our brokenness.

So, what would happen if we look at chaos or endings or brokenness as an invitation? What difference would it make if we saw the cracks that chaos renders as a way to open up to the light? What would happen if we repositioned chaos as an energy that invites us to recreate, soften, and energize our workplaces, homes, communities, and even ourselves?

Looking at the chaos of life this way does not mean we will avoid suffering and grief. This life does not work that way. It does not mean that we become chaos cheerleaders with a false cheerfulness and toxic positivity overlooking the fact that our team has been decimated. It *does* mean we begin to forge a path through the chaos, accepting life on life's terms and finding ways to incorporate our struggles into a renewed wholeness.

Over the years, I have witnessed leaders embrace chaos, ride with the changes, and channel uncertainty to deepen connections as they feel their feelings and learn more about themselves. Organizations comfortable with chaos are the most innovative and game-changing. Husbands and wives who are comfortable with chaos realize they have the capacity to stand together on sacred ground, turn toward each other, enhancing vulnerability instead of blame. Individuals who risk vulnerability with trusted people find out what it is like to be accepted for who they truly are as they grow more into their most whole selves.

How can we see the creative energies that reside with the chaos? How can we stop trying to keep things the same and step into change with an attitude of possibility? My friend Nick's words fill me every time I falter, every time I look chaos in the face, every time I wonder which road to take: "If nothing changes, nothing changes."

The Gift of the Horizon: Spotting Chaos in Advance

Somedays I want to beat chaos back. Build stronger walls. Divert it so my life remains untouched. Cut it off at the pass. Throw a super-sized tantrum.

However, we can no more stop chaos from coming into our lives than we can sprinkle fairy dust on the heartache of our children; we can, however, become more mindful and, as a result, more able to see chaos approaching at times. Sometimes, chaos takes us completely by surprise.

And yet, sometimes our own denial prevents us from accepting its stealthy approach. If we can face life's obvious challenges with more acceptance and less denial, we can better prepare ourselves to deal with chaos and its accompanying painful consequences, whether we are facing barbarians at the gate or family upheaval. Not all stress, anxiety, and change can be avoided, so creating a certain kind of awareness within our lives can certainly minimize it and break through self-deception.

The best leaders in the boardroom, community, and household have a sense of where chaos might originate, what feeds it, and how to create strong antibodies to fight it or soften it when it does arise. Take two examples.

One head of human resources realized that a certain executive in the organization, responsible for critical financial successes, was also responsible for a consistent amount of bullying and verbally abusive behavior. It was demoralizing and demotivating to many in the organization, and instead of waiting for the inevitable lawsuit to manifest, she took action: addressing the situation, finding solutions, and ensuring that the organization and employees were protected while the executive was given a variety of ways that he could successfully change his behavior. By accepting the situation instead of denying it, the human resources executive created a proactive approach which prevented more chaos from occurring.

On the other hand, in a different organization, there was a similar situation: an executive with a history of solid results was also demoralizing her employees. The CEO knew about this behavior and was reluctant to truly address it. Other top executives were concerned about addressing the situation because the company did not have many women in the top echelon. Their excuses for not addressing the situation were fueled for a long time; they had a weak rationale every time an employee came forward. Eventually, they were sued and had to deal with a tremendous amount of negative fallout because they choose denial over acceptance, inaction over proactive responses.

By understanding what gives life to chaos and paying attention to the signs, we can often strengthen our ability to be more in touch with what is happening around us and within us. Preparing ourselves for the inevitable chaos is best done when things are going smoothly. Do not wait until the thing comes that will shake your foundation. The map through is best studied in advance, our perseverance best shored up by strengthening our practices that create wellbeing when life is calmer.

Some of the most effective ways of preparing ourselves for chaos lie in the basics:

Staying Awake. Those who are able to sense change and disruption coming are often loving warriors at home and work, focused on honing their intuition. Like Michael Jordan, they can see the play before it happens. They have keen insight into others. They trust their gut. They can discern bullshit when many of us are talking too loudly to even notice it. They do this naturally because they are comfortable with what they know and who they are. They accept the truth about others' behaviors and do not hide behind wishful thinking. They listen to the ancient voice within during calm times so they can recognize it above the din.

Remaining Connected. Those who sense chaos coming and learn from its wisdom know how to connect with self, others, and a higher spiritual energy. They benefit from having daily practices that strengthen their self-awareness. They draw supportive energy from a circle of people willing to cheer them on and who are vulnerable right alongside them. Even in their most terrifying moments, those courageous enough to reach out to others with honesty fare better and even thrive.

Welcoming Rhythm. People who have finely tuned discernment have practices that allow them to tune in to themselves physically, emotionally, relationally, spiritually, and mentally. When people can sense what is going on beneath the water line, they are less surprised when something from below crashes through to the surface. This type of rhythm is the simple act of finding harmony, experiencing oneness, and creating a life in tune with all that surrounds us so we are as prepared as possible to navigate the tough times.

Doing the Next Right Thing. Doing the right thing makes life easier and can limit self-created chaos. When we do the next wrong thing, chaos almost always ensues. The rules for what can make middle school a bit easier apply to all of life:

- *Follow the rules.* Develop a reputation for being a collaborator and not a troublemaker. Understand that the guardrails are there for a reason; life flows more easily when we stay between them and are known as trustworthy.
- *Ask good questions.* Learn the skill of raising issues respectfully. It is okay to question the rules, but only after one masters them. By adhering to the playbook and doing so effectively we earn the right to raise questions about whether or not there is a better way, a wiser way, or a more courageous, connected way to navigate any given situation.
- *Lift others up.* We are all in this together. Remember, it is okay not to like someone, and it is healthy to set clear boundaries with people who lie, tear others down, lash out at us, are not willing to be accountable, or abuse and betray us. It is *not* okay to be mean, bully, spread rumors, gossip, and throw temper tantrums to manipulate someone or a situation.
- *Be concerned about others' wellbeing.* You will feel more support when you support others. This is not a foolproof plan, as haters will most likely always hate, whether you show concern for their wellbeing or not. But in the end, your empathy will strengthen you, and banner-waving people will cheer you on. Run toward those folks and ensure you behave and speak in ways that are true, kind, and necessary.
- *Teamwork matters.* Acknowledge that you need help, accept it when offered, ask for it often, and celebrate that you have a village to turn to. This is not a do-it-yourself life.

Being Present. People are not projects to manage. They do not open up on schedule because you have given them fifteen minutes on your calendar. Children talk about their lives when you are in the kitchen fixing a meal, driving them home from practice, hanging out. In those natural moments, the magic happens. Employees are more apt to tell you what is on their minds when you regularly make yourself available and do so in environments conducive to relaxation. A spouse is more apt to talk about what is on their mind when you are focused on them over a relaxing dinner or enjoying an activity together. I once heard someone say that they had been there for someone enduring a heart-wrenching time by liking their Facebook posts. People! Liking a social media post does not count as being present!

These suggestions are some of the most meaningful ways to reduce self-created chaos. Once you begin to practice them regularly, they will eventually become habitual and make life more harmonious. Becoming comfortable with chaos is essential, because though chaos does not last forever, it always returns eventually. And we want to be prepared with faith, hope, strength, and grace to face it.

We become what we do. We strengthen what we practice.

The Education within Chaos

Chaos is a butt kicker. And it takes great delight in kicking us again while we lie on the ground trying to recover from the first blow. It is often difficult to get up and maybe we don't even want to. We think, "What is the use after all?" It would be easier to crumple in the corner with our blankie in hand. Yet chaos brings us face to face with what all great literature teaches: within the loss and challenge, we find redemption and purpose.

A sign in our kitchen says, "We do hard things." It does not say, "We like doing hard things." It should say, "Momma goes kicking and screaming into doing hard things." It is a reminder that, within reason, when we push ourselves out of our comfort zone, we trust that hidden in the hard thing we will find wisdom.

This is leadership. This is welcoming the chaos. This is a foundation for connection.

I know the chaos that comes from "everything is fine" one minute to "everything is terrifying" the next. That sort of chaos will stop you in your tracks and put you on the floor, which is literally where my husband and I wound up that afternoon in a hotel room in Ohio when the call came from my doctor that I had breast cancer. It was not the first or last time that chaos and grief literally yanked the rug out from underneath me and brought me to my knees.

Life is messy, personally and professionally. Therefore, it is critical that we lead with our integrated selves: mind, body, heart, soul. Doing so allows us to become the hands that work on others, the friendly forces, the gentle encourager that stands stronger as a result of the chaos navigated.

Connection Reflection: Navigates Chaos

o   Start with yourself. Craft time and space to explore what has broken you wide open. Share this exploration with a trusted guide or friend so that you can become even more spiritually and emotionally awake as a leader at work and at home.

o   When disruptions or disappointments or challenges occur at work, how do you want to show up? What can you do during the calm, smooth times to prepare yourself to show up in those ways?

o   What have you learned about yourself as a result of the chaos and grief you have gone through? How have those times made you more of your true self? Is there something getting in the way that you need to work through.

Chapter Eight

Walks with Confidence: Courage Raises Us Up

"To be courageous is not necessarily to go anywhere or do anything except to make conscious those things we already feel deeply and then to live through the unending vulnerabilities of those consequences."
—David Whyte

Most of us want to be perceived as being confident. When we are in the presence of someone who is confident, they seem comfortable in their own skin. They know they are good at certain things. They are direct, easy to be with. Being around someone who is this kind of confident helps others to feel at ease like they are in good hands and that things will go smoothly.

By working with executives and their teams, I have come to identify two types of confidence. One is the kind that results from having a history of success doing certain tasks quite well. This is what I refer to as *functional confidence*. We know what we need to know to do our job. We are well-versed in the nuts and bolts of our craft. We know what we are doing, so to speak, and are clear that we are masterful and well-respected because of it. This gives a leader what she needs to go up in front of a committee of venture capitalists and present her business plan. The second is the kind of confidence that comes from believing deep within that we are strong, persevering, and resilient because of the struggles we have experienced. This is what I refer to as *courage-based confidence*. It is based on knowing what we are made of. It gives an executive the energy and grit to testify in the largest antitrust case ever or be the one that others seek out for encouragement when the deal is dying on the vine.

Courage-based confidence is what allows Kyle Maynard, a quadruple amputee, to ascend Mount Kilimanjaro without using prosthetics. It is what allows a mother to say goodbye to her fourteen-year-old as he leaves to spend an entire summer, out of contact with her, backpacking through Maine to discover his inner strength. It is what propelled Molly Fletcher, a friend of mine and an extraordinarily successful former sports agent, to leave that career in order to follow her dream of becoming a highly sought-after motivational speaker.

When it comes to being a Connected Leader, the kind of confidence I am talking about is completely aligned with courage. Bold. Heart-bearing. Dig-down-deep, vulnerable courage. To rise up knowing we survived the wilderness, thrived in spite of bullies within and outside of us, discovered treasures buried deep inside, and eventually let our light loose to shine in the world.

At age thirteen, my son told me over lunch that he wanted to go to boarding school. I grabbed hold of the sides of the table and white-knuckled it. I wanted to say, "Over my dead body." But I managed to say, "Can you tell me more?" He knew what he wanted and needed. Even then, more so than me, he was brave. This is what he said: "I need a hero's journey. I need to know who I am apart from you."

And so he went. During his boarding school experience, he woke up to parts of himself he needed to examine, and parts worth celebrating.

What Is Confidence?

In our driven, goal-oriented, get-as-much-as-you-can world, we typically view confidence as the ability to take on challenging assignments or boldly assert one's opinion. We push ourselves continually while seeking outward signs of our competence and worthiness. We yearn to be recognized as a success based on skills we have mastered.

We need this skill-based confidence to do the things our lives require of us, but if confidence stops there and is not balanced with the other attributes of a Connected Leader, it can morph into an ego-driven arrogance, a narcissistic, insatiable need for more power and more approval.

Our culture is more familiar with skill-based confidence. If we don't broaden the definition of confidence to also include courage-based confidence, we will remain stuck: stuck in thinking that confidence comes from creating outputs others can applaud as opposed to it also coming from an inward journey that only we can experience.

So, here we go: courage-based confidence enhances a sense of belonging to ourselves and, as a consequence, strengthens our community. It comes from doing our inner emotional and spiritual work, of moving beyond our fears, surrendering to powerlessness, leaning into all emotions, accepting painful truths about ourselves, choosing meaningfulness, and embracing our gifts in order to have the impact on the world we are designed to have.

Courage-based confidence provides people with a sense of contentment, self-acceptance, and endurance; it shows us that whatever life throws at us, we can handle it with honesty and graciousness. Let's be clear, though. This is not a sugary sweet, overly simplistic, falsely positive approach to life's frustrations and heartbreak; beating ourselves up for not being positive enough only mires us in self-blame when we don't see everything as unicorns and rainbows.

Rather, this is a confidence that comes from trusting yourself, because you know you have triumphed before and you will rise up again. This is not about positivity; this is about being real and leaning into the struggles in a way that is authentic so that you and other people come to trust you even more. It is what allows a cancer survivor to wait for the results of her yearly tests without completely losing it while she waits. It is what encourages an executive to show up genuinely and honest to talk with her team about the upcoming merger: the second in five years. It is what allows the entrepreneur to show up to a client call two days after his son recovers from a major health care.

Courage-based confidence, however, is a tough partner; it gives generously and expects everything in return. Yes, it teaches us to trust our internal reserves as we walk in faith. It allows us to move with grace when anxiety kicks in—when the relationship ends, the termination is really happening, or we don't know how we will make ends meet. It strengthens us to look within and admit our flaws, talk about our wounds to people who have earned our trust, and remain open even when life is unraveling. It holds us together when we are exhausted, under attack, depleted.

However, courage-based confidence expects certain things in return; it is an exacting gift-giver. It expects that we will possess rigorous self-honesty and vulnerability. It expects that we will seek out experiences that grow and stretch us, be the warrior we know we can be, and marry hard-earned skill with emotional and spiritual strength. It teaches us to remain steadfast by accepting what is *and* trusting that, in acceptance, there can be important shifts and even miracles.

People who have not yet developed courage-based confidence have difficulty having an intimate conversation with themselves about what is working and what could be different. Of course, they do…because it is hard. Stinkin' hard. This kind of examination has the potential of turning everything topsy-turvy as we move away from entrenched patterns, denial, and enter into the truth and uncertainty that comes with doing life differently.

Here is the thing: until we let go of those things that keep us stuck, we are not going to be courageous and free enough to live our most meaningful lives, and thus create our most joyful relationships. We cannot step into and relish our purpose, serving others from a healthy sense of wellbeing, until we let go of the tried-and-true-but-limiting and give ourselves to something that brings us a sense of purposeful, all-in meaning.

Even the relatively simple act of not being at other people's beck-and-call when they want something from me can cause me to breathe shallowly and feel a bit queasy. Learning that I do not have to respond to every angry word, emotional demand, crazy blame-game, or even a reasonable request is one of the shifts that fuel my inner courage-based confidence as I lean into the truth that I am more than an eternal spring for others.

As Parker Palmer states so beautiful in his most recent book, On the Brink of Everything,

> *"I no longer ask, 'What do I want to let go of and what do I want to hang onto?' Instead, I ask, 'What do I want to let go of, and what do I want to give myself to?'"*[30]

I suggest that courage-based confidence is one of the things we give ourselves to. It is one of the empowering strategies of connection: one of the beautiful gifts that allow us to connect more deeply with our true selves, our purpose, and as a result, connect more meaningfully to others which loops us back, of course, to deepening our connection with ourselves and the God of our understanding.

This work is not for the fainthearted. Facing our fears and un-packing how we have kept ourselves defended yet defeated will free us, but not before it dismantles the comfort zone we have built. It feels easier to stay cozying-up to the coping skills known by many: blaming, shaming, attacking, denying. They might not be effective, but they are what is known, and they can keep us quite entertained with a misguided sense of power and protection.

As an example, denial is like that so-called friend we all have. Someone who activates our insecure self and encourages us to do things not in our best interest: things and behaviors that keep us in a trance, and even sometimes, places us in dangerous situations.

Most of us know, on some level, what to run toward and what to stay away from; but when denial kicks in and we are allowing ourselves to be directed away from our center, it can convince us that "yes, this is good…not a problem." And while addiction is a sharply clear example of denial's power, it is not by any stretch the only time that we human beings choose what is unhealthy over what is life-affirming.

So despite a leader's ability to command the stage, close the deal, run the race, or score the goal, the real litmus test is whether or not they can walk into their inner world and examine their feelings, histories, and ways of thinking so they can heal, awaken, and courageously lead unfettered by denial or the tempting calls of modern-day sirens. It might look like many people who occupy powerful positions lead, but many a leader is filled with unexamined insecurities, and as a consequence, is easily triggered and seduced by whatever calls him or her. People who lack courage-based confidence might get things done, yet eventually they easily lose their way when temptation beckons—emboldened by their own unexamined motives instead of focusing on the something more that is required.

The something more is the ability to navigate life's impermanence, choose wisely, and live meaningfully. The something more is digging deep into our inner worlds and accepting our struggles with darkness, control, resentments, and unhealthy agendas. Courage-based confidence does not guarantee that life will be great every day; it does, however, mean that when life and work unexpectedly rear-ends us, we learn to respond gracefully, powerfully, and honestly in a way that inspires others instead of creating even more of a mess for ourselves and others. And I guess that is pretty great after all.

A Profile in Courage

Jackie maintains a daunting list of accomplishments, including serving as a captain in the Air Force and working in a variety of high-pressure, top-level positions in numerous organizations. She is a force of nature who leads from the front and connects to those who work with her in ways that leave others remarking on her presence, intelligence, and warmth. During a recent conversation, Jackie shared with me how she has come to embrace courage-based confidence in her life and work:

> "I have been much more transparent, open, and vulnerable as my career has gone on. When I struggle now, I ask for help instead of continuing to be stuck in the struggle and just trying to survive. I share what my life is like, including what it is like to have Eric, my husband, at home as his eye disease progresses and neither one of us knows what the future holds."

Decades ago, Jackie had an opportunity to work in Europe. She planned to tell them no. She could not see how it would work with three young children and a husband whose work was also important to him. However, when she told her husband her plan, he replied: "You tell them, 'Hell yes.' I will quit my job, and the family will work to support this opportunity you have." He never looked back after that statement. Now, as his vision fades from disease, her response to Eric years later is, "Hell yes, I am here beside you."

As David Whyte, poet and philosopher writes, "Courage is what love looks like when tested by the simple everyday necessities of being alive."[31] Courage invites us to go deeper into love and grief, different sides of the same coin; it invites us to go deeper into our own yearnings and regret, daily challenges, and ordinary acts of bravery. Courage is contagious and strengthening, it is not without fear and it tells us we are stronger than we thought. And that, is what our people, our spouses, our children, and communities need to know: that courage will allow us to say, like Jackie and Eric have, "hell yes."

The Quiet of Courage-Based Confidence

I am a big fan of quiet, stillness, and humility. It is difficult to keep this focus as we live in the culture of comparison, exacerbated by the onslaught of selfies and self-promotion. The sense of urgency that all this activity can stir up deeply impacts me at times. I often say to my team and friends, "I woke up this morning feeling like I'm missing out on an opportunity, a chance to prove myself, to say what needs to be said, and build our firm. Other people are doing it quicker, noisier, and with, what seems to be, more speed and support." It can leave me feeling worthless, scared, and critical that I am not doing enough, fast enough, well enough.

During these times, I slow down, go quiet, stay focused, and dig deep to be courageous, and as a consequence, confident. It can sometimes feel like I am pushing water uphill so I want to be clear that none of this is easy. However, I remind myself that I can in fact finish writing this book. I can walk out on that stage. I do have something to add when I am talking with clients in the C-suite. And I can stand strong yet gentle as I have difficult conversations. I can choose to hit the pause button and tend to family over work.

I can do these things, and often do, but I want people to know that it is not as effortless and easy as it seems. Many moments, I torture myself in the privacy of my own world with feelings of "not being enough" to enough people quickly enough. After these moments pass, often after healing solitude and connecting conversations with people who truly know me, I move on with more of this courage-based confidence.

Connected Leaders who possess the ability to walk with confidence know what they are good at. They also move through life believing in their inner strength and do so without much fanfare. They let their work and spirit speak for themselves. But the ability to walk with confidence comes because we are real about our fears, personally and professionally.

So, here are seven guidelines to develop and live from a courage-based confidence:

- **Trust you were designed to have a hero's journey.** To have a hero's journey means leaving the known and comfortable to wrestle with the unknown for a larger good. We seek transformation not just in our own lives but for others as well, even if we are not sure what that means when we start the journey. We feel a call, an itch, a desire to leave the ordinary to find the extraordinary. Being a true hero is about accepting one's woundedness, healing from that, and passing the wisdom learned onto others. As Joseph Campbell so eloquently stated, "We have only to follow the thread of the hero path. Where we had thought to find an abomination, we shall find a god; where we had thought to slay another, we shall slay ourselves; where we had thought to travel outwards, we shall come to the center of our own existence; where we had thought to be alone, we shall be with all the world."[32]

- **You have triumphed before, and you will do so again.** There is nothing like recalling how resilient you were after a past mistake, or when you were in the presence of a bully, or when you were scraped to the bone with a heartbreak to trust you can flourish again. Rising up rewires the brain and becomes embedded in our DNA. We forget that the story is unearthed in the struggle. Yes, people want to hear about the triumph, but only because there first was a huge barrier to break through.

I was facilitating a leadership retreat for the top fifteen leaders of one of Georgia's largest engineering firms. We were discussing the Southwest plane incident in which the pilot, Tammie Jo Shults, landed a jet with only one engine. We discussed all the training she had completed, focusing on chaos and emergencies since her time as a Navy pilot, but we also touched significantly on what had to be her courage-based confidence. She had been in tight situations before and somehow that had become a part of her DNA. The CEO of the engineering firm, Jay Wolverton, put it this way: "I don't want to take anything away from how dire the situation was and how skilled she was. It is amazing, really. But what happened is she used her past experiences with struggles and her training to turn the unspeakable into a matter-of-fact incident. It became,

'We just happen to be landing a jet that has one hole in it,' as opposed to 'Oh my God, we are going to crash.'"

- **Dig down deep into what you have learned.** We possess a wealth of wisdom garnered over a lifetime of lessons, but we don't always employ that wisdom, so we create the same blessed mess over and over.

  Many of us do not trust that we have all we need inside of us, and so the endless journey begins to seek the solutions outside of ourselves. As we continue to look outside of ourselves, we give up our power and wisdom in the hope that someone or something else—anyone or anything else—will come and save us. The God I have come to know wants us to be a partner in our growth and healing, even if it just means being honest and praying one of the most powerful of prayers: "Help!"

  Anne Lamott, in all of her irreverent humor and ability to simply nail it, says this: "It's funny: I always imagined when I was a kid that adults had some kind of inner toolbox full of shiny tools: the saw of discernment, the hammer of wisdom, the sandpaper of patience. But then when I grew up I found that life handed you these rusty bent old tools—friendships, prayer, conscience, honesty—and said 'Do the best you can with these, they will have to do.' And mostly, against all odds, they do."[33]

- **Know the power of your gifts.** Our gifts go way beyond our degrees, no-hitters pitched, GPAs, bylines, and corporate titles. Our gifts show up in the everyday give and take of creating a life and embracing who we are in the face of our perfect imperfections and shadowy light; our power lies in accepting our contradictions and humanness, our complexities and nuances. We often find this kind of surrendering-power in the stirring of the oatmeal, in the mindful moments when we are conscious that everything belongs, as we humble ourselves so we can find our true strength, and as we help those we love attend to their healing by giving them tough and loving feedback. At the intersection of our mess and someone else's ache or question, we can put our gifts to work as we find ways to use them to connect to others.

- **If it does not work, it does not mean "it" or you are a failure.** Picture the tendency many of us have to beat ourselves up for decisions made, people dated, jobs taken, money spent, and words spoken. As we dismantle ourselves through this self-loathing, we miss the opportunity to learn and enhance our inner confidence. In leadership as in life, failure can be heart-wrenching, but if we live so carefully that we don't fail, we have failed.

- **Say "Hell yes."** I was raised by a mother who was so overcome with anxiety that she eventually did not leave the house or talk to other people out of fear that she would say the wrong thing. Her fears had nothing to do with who she truly was—smart, funny, warm-hearted, articulate, and thoughtful—but they dictated the design of her life. The echo of her fear lives within me. How could it not? But I have been fortunate enough to be surrounded by people who inspire me to live big in every way, even if "no" is still the first thing I imagine hearing from others and remains my own internal reflex. It is the "hell yes" that takes us from the safe to the fully lived, from the status quo to the extraordinary.

- **Be you, not them: do not hustle for outward approval.** I am a self-admitted recovering approval junkie. When you are an approval junkie you wind up hustling constantly in the hope that you will finally be seen as competent and worthy so you can stop approval-seeking. The problem becomes exacerbated, because competency breeds more competency: then comes the applause and bylines, promotions and rewards. Except like with any junkie, it is never enough, so we get worn down, depleted, and exhausted. It is never enough—until we are sick and tired of being sick and tired and do the hard, hard work of going inward; resting; listening deeply; being present, not perfect; and saying no.

As I continue learning to be me and not "them," to enjoy me and not please them, I have a little secret: I can be a badass. I am a warrior. And I like those sides of myself that are not as focused as they used to be on ensuring that everyone else around me is whistlin' zippity-do-dah.

As Warren Bennis said, "Becoming a leader is synonymous with becoming yourself. It's precisely that simple, and it's also that difficult."[34]

And so the path of courage-based confidence is right in front of us. It truly is a road less traveled. It is a road that has more detours than straight passages and leads us into the wilderness, where we find what we have spent too much time looking for elsewhere: ourselves. Once we find that, leading others is the easier part in a lot of ways.

Connection Reflection: Walks with Confidence

o   Go through the seven tips to develop an ability to walk with confidence. Journal about them. Learn how you dig deep and rise up.
o   Often times, we get the same lesson over and over again until we change what we can change. And as the lessons repeat, they show up with more intensity until they crescendo into a crisis designed to get our attention (finally!). How can you embrace courage now so that you don't have to experience a crisis to do something different?

Chapter Nine

And So...

"In the end, we do not so much reclaim what we have lost as discover a significantly new self in and through the process. Until we are led to the limits of our present game plan and find it insufficient, we will not search out or find the real source, the deep well, or the constantly flowing stream."

—Richard Rohr, *Falling Upward:*
A Spirituality for the Two Halves of Life

Life is full of endings and beginnings—some so subtle that we do not really recognize the transition until we look in the rearview mirror. Some so knock-us-on-our-butts powerful that we do not know how the hell we are going to make it to the ending, never mind begin again.

As this book-writing process comes to an end, it comes as no surprise to me that many other endings dovetail with it. The universe is funny that way. It likes to create a cosmic dogpile so we don't miss the lesson.

For me, life's recent transitions have been plentiful: moving out of one house and into another (right up there with experiencing a death according to stress experts—what were we thinking?), my husband semi-retiring (on the stress scales right up there with death and moving—really, what the hell were we thinking?), and the writing of this book soon coming to an end.

Obviously, I like to pour it on sometimes: if one transition is stressful, let's supersize the transitions and get as much of the shit kicked out of us as possible in one fell swoop.

As with all things, it is sometimes tough to say, "Now. Now I am done. I have done well, learned a ton, time to move on." It is also a time to wonder, "Have I done enough? Said enough? Is it really time to end this thing and move on?"

So, it is with this book, which has served much like an alchemist for me. It is time to let it go, to say, "It is enough."

Therefore, it has been a tough, anxious time for me emotionally, and it has also been a joyful, empowering time for me emotionally. One is not better than the other. I am trying to get better at that—not judging one set of emotions as bad and the other set as good. I am just trying to name how I experience all of life at any one moment. How deeply I am connected to myself and to the God of my understanding is what determines, at any moment, if I am seeing it as a tough or joyful week…or maybe just both.

Then this happened: a conversation with my friend Barri Rafferty who is former CEO of Ketchum and currently Head of Communications and Brand Management for Wells Fargo.

We started talking about courage-based confidence, but the roots of the conversation, like the roots of the aspens, reached out and formed connections with the other six strategies of being a Connected Leader: you can't talk about courage-based confidence without talking about listening deeply, being empathetic, and being vulnerable. They all operate as one interconnected whole, flowing into each other and strengthening each other.

As I sat on my screened-in porch listening to Barri, I tuned into her stories of her children coming home from college, having a full house, and going grocery shopping. Though she is a world-class executive, Barri will always, first and foremost, be real. Therefore, it comes as no surprise that she intentionally cultivates being a Connected Leader. She says:

> "Leaders set the weather. Emotions are contagious, and through their communications, attitudes, behaviors, and body language, leaders are sending constant messages all the time that others take on. I spend time truly developing and listening to my inner voice so I can set the weather in a way that inspires others and myself."

Those of us who lead at home and/or in the workplace, decide on a daily basis if our people need to put on a rain jacket or take cover in a tornado shelter because of the storms we create...or if they can shine in the sunlight because of how we show up.

So. Chase slow. Dig deep. Rise up. Discover your power and true self throughout this messy, zigzaggy process. Find your own internal deep well. And teach others to do the same through your inspiration.

We are moving out of traditional leadership paradigms and into the type of leadership that flows from our inner work. The kind of leadership that moves us into the Connection Era strengthened by our intentional vulnerability, purposeful stories, and fully human authenticity.

And Then There Is This...

Remember what I said earlier in this chapter? About all those big changes?

There was one more change hiding in the shadows. It would show its face ever so slightly and then sneak back into the darkness, maybe because we were not quite ready for it, maybe because it was not quite yet ready for us. It was a change that was getting bolder over a few months' time, preparing to show itself in full.

My husband, son, and I visited Colorado with my family. We stayed in a beautiful resort that made it easy for us to be together, typically over food, on hiking trails, and sitting next to the creek.

I rose early one morning, wrapped myself in a blanket, and had my coffee by the stream. No one else was up. Not long after I settled in, a herd of elks meandered down the mountain, stopping slowly along the way to eat, graze, and wade in the brook. I was mesmerized by how they walked slowly, in step with each other, with such intention. I was so taken by this once in a lifetime experience that I had no clue that elk can also trample humans.

It was just me—the lone human—and about thirty-five mama elks and their babies. One came so close to me that we looked into each other's eyes, holding each other's gaze for a few seconds before Mama Elk turned her enormous head and walked toward her buddies. I felt as if she was trying to tell me something; I can still see her eyes as I write this.

I wanted to know more about these animals and why, in that moment, they crossed my path. What was the message they carried? Afterward, I learned that Native American people believed that when elk crossed your path, it was to remind you of how important it is to pace yourself on your journey, especially during times of overwhelm and uncertainty. They also remind us that connection and community are of the utmost importance in order to persevere.

Mama Elk was trying to tell me something. I know that now.

Shortly after we returned from Colorado, our life as we knew it unraveled. My husband, whose struggles had been manifesting for a few months, received a diagnosis of Alzheimer's. It explained a great deal. It shatters us still.

It has been a long six months since we received the diagnosis. The ineffable grief and life-altering losses impact us every day, individually and together as a married couple. The vows we took resound in my mind; who knew during our day of joy and dancing, cake and shiny things, celebration and sacred togetherness that our vow of "in sickness and health" would carry such meaning? That so much would be required? That the normal wear and tear, the daily negotiations, would take such a back seat to this rip-the-heart-out shattering?

We are deep in the deep end, pushed in, far from the shallows. And as we learn to float in this terrifying depth where our feet can't touch, we are also given moments of tremendous grace and sweetness and connection. We are surrounded by a most giving, true, and supportive circle of devoted friends and family who strengthen us and keep us afloat when sometimes we are too exhausted and about to go under. I stay close to my recovery and healing, my solitude and prayer, my work and those sources of nourishing energy.

And as if the Alzheimer's diagnosis was not enough, I learned that a beloved person in my life needed rehab, immediately; and so, in the midst of visits to the Alzheimer's facility, I was also upping my twelve step game to deal with the onslaught of addiction's insanity.

God must think I am a colossal badass.

Because of these bring-us-to-our-knees heartbreaks, the attributes I talk about in this book took on an even more transformative meaning. My son and I strengthened our connection to each other and our tribe; these relationships became even more loving and sweeter. My work with executives all around the globe grew to be even more transformative. Sometimes it takes this type of grief and loss to make those of us interested in healthy growth become better, more honest, open, and willing.

When he was still able, my husband would check in with me and ask me how this book was progressing; I would tell him "it is so very close to being done." He knew how excruciatingly difficult it had been to make my work and writing a priority as the plates underneath my feet shifted in cataclysmic ways. A people-pleaser of Olympic proportions, I was now enrolled in a master class of self-care, boundary setting, and self-compassion, which is part of the core curriculum for connection. Courtesy of my husband's disease and my choice to walk the recovery walk with a beloved, I was being offered the lesson of my lifetime: take care of your emotional and spiritual wellbeing first so you can pace yourself and help others do the same on their journey.

The disruptions I had viewed as barriers to completing this book were actual treasures. As it turns out, the finishing of this book had not been delayed but remade with even more meaning.

And so, the Mama Elk who made eye contact with me did have a message. Without sounding too "out there" or "woo-woo," I know she and her herd crossed my path that morning for a reason. Less than a year after that, the great thief of Alzheimer's would steal my husband slowly...and then quickly. And the dragon call of addiction would rear its head. It is no coincidence that Mama Elk gifted me that morning with two reminders. One, she symbolized the need to persevere and two, to do so in the context of community and connection.

As I navigate this journey, I ground myself in the power of my herd, the wisdom of those who walk before me, and the divine presence that restores me to sanity and whose care I surrender to every day.

Connected Leaders are at the center of a revolution, whether we are learning to float in the deep end, guide our herd down a mountain, surrender to the first step, or inspire a boardroom.

Connected Leaders chase slow, dig deep, and rise up. Amen.

Epilogue/Afterword

Two days after I got word from my wonderful agent, John Willig, that my book was under contract by my publisher, my husband did not recognize me, a moment I knew would come. I knew I would not be the exception to how his disease works; no one was or is. No one is special or unique enough to sidestep that inevitability. I knew it despite his best friend, Bill, once saying, "I don't think he will ever forget you. You are the love of his life." I knew it through all the tough, chaotic, despairing days during which my husband clung to me and lit up when I walked in.

Six months into dating me, Greg said, "I want to be with you until the Good Lord takes me home." I will never forget his words or where we were when he said them; they took my breath away, because speaking that way was not like him. He was a tough street kid from Cleveland turned CPA: more comfortable with numbers than with poetry. Even more reason why I never forgot what he said.

I have run as hard as I can to connection my whole life. The irony doesn't escape me: I teach connection. I crave connection. And now, in some twisted cosmic joke, the universe says, "How do you like this for a punchline? You, the lover of connection, were not recognized."

I have grieved Greg in private, and with my circle, for a long time: pieces of him I once counted on stripped away over long days, hopeless nights, and many moons, layer by layer. As he slipped into more and more of a world occupied by just him, I still remember everything, which is both helpful and torturous. When I first started dating Greg, I remember saying to a friend, "I walk through my days feeling utterly protected, trusting, not at all uncertain." This is what Greg wanted me to know: that he was, in his essence, steady, certain, sure-footed, and safe. Despite the relentless nature of how his disease robbed him and us, I keep connected to what he hoped I would always believe: his presence was a strong and unwavering one.

As I ugly-cried that morning with my golden retriever's paw never leaving my arm, this is what I concluded (because how else does any of life's crazy messiness and heartbreak makes sense?):

1. We are made for connection, and it is for always. When we connect deeply and in healthy ways, we release the best in ourselves and others, regardless of how life's darkness might twist the ever-lovin' snot out of us. God knew exactly what He was doing when He wired us for connection. He really did. And as leaders at work and in life, we need to keep running to connection, using the seven strategies as connection-activators even on days when it feels like it is slipping through our fingers.

2. On days when connection does slip through our fingers, God is always there, never leaving. He is the ultimate connection and connector. We can count on that, and as we leave behind the ridiculous notion that the ultimate power resides within us and accept that there is a power greater than ourselves, connection deepens in spades. Truly. Crazily. No exception. And this is what brings others to believe in the transformative power of connection.

3. Connection is not necessarily based on what we can touch and see. Connection—true connection—happens in the soul and exists forever, even though our ego-driven desire for appreciation and recognition is sometimes painfully wounded when we are forgotten...or devalued...or rejected...or left behind.

4. Connection is about creating and holding sacred space even when you might be the only one conscious and intentional about doing so. And, as we do so even on the darkest days, we keep a light on for others. They feel it. It guides them. And, this is God, too, shining through us.

Later that morning, after my husband did not recognize me, Matthew called and asked me how my day was going; I told him it was okay. He noticed my silence. His voice dropped, "What happened, Mom?" I wondered if I should say anything: you know that struggle between protection and the truth when it comes to our children. However, I voted for vulnerability, bravery, and connection and said, "Dad did not know me this morning."

And then the deep rootedness kicked in, the sacred lifeblood of connection flowed, and Matthew, our son, with so many important things to do, said to his mother (me), "I will be right there." I told him not to come. But he insisted, and so I let him choose.

And in that nanosecond, I knew it was deep inside of Matthew, too: the power of connection.

A few months later, my husband, Greg, died. Five days before he passed, I was sitting with him and played one of his favorite songs; he connected to it immediately, even though he was no longer talking. And I was not surprised at all; he sang some of the lyrics and then held his hand out to dance; and as he sat, eyes closed, I danced with him. That was the last time he interacted with this world in a clear way.

Given his love for music and dancing and me, it made sense that this was his last truly intentional act. As my brother would say, it is entirely possible Greg was the fifth Top. He knew every word to every song written since the 1950s. He could also name the artist, the song-writers' names, their parents' names, the street on which the song was recorded, and what the artists ate for dinner the night after cutting the record. Whether we were driving down the streets of Charleston or at sporting events, he sang because he could not not sing. It was the way he connected to the joy inside of him.

Four days before Greg passed, Matthew, spoke to about 250 people about the healing power of connection to self, others, and God. I told Greg about it afterward; he would have been so proud to see Matthew speaking in public so powerfully. It was one of the very few times Greg opened his eyes in recognition during his final days, and the only time he squeezed my hand. As Greg was making his transition, the power of connection held and the center strengthened.

I spent his final days—nearly around the clock—walking Greg home, creating a sacred space and knowing that he was doing pro-found soul-work as his body gave up its work. It was a spiritual experience that had one focus and one focus only: ensuring he felt loved, released, encouraged, and grieved over. It was the longest consistent God-moment I ever had. It was made of all the important pieces of connection as family called to say their goodbyes and share their appreciation with him, friends sent texts that I read to him, our son kept the vigil prayerfully, and I repeated our favorite prayers and read his favorite scripture to him.

And yet, the most important connection was what was happening deep inside of Greg. As only a spouse can know. A spouse who knows the true essence of their partner's heart. I knew he knew. I knew he and I were sharing an intimacy that we had prepared for over many a year, many a conversation, many a struggle, and many soul connections. He knew I was walking him home, and I knew he and I were working together to give him his heart's desire: to be with me, and totally so, until the Good Lord called him home.

Years before, when I got to the finish line of the New York Marathon, Greg asked me what marathon I was going to run next, since he had run many. My look said it all: there would be no other marathons for me. But I was wrong.

There *was* another marathon: a grueling, brutal one that took all we had, one we ran together until the end. And one in which the theme of connection took on a whole new meaning: connection to self, God, and others in the face of disconnection.

Greg got his heart's desire. He was with me until the Good Lord called him home, on a rainy morning in Georgia, after I poured out my heart and told him what I knew he needed to hear, as the cardinals chirped outside his window, and his music played in the background. It was well with his soul, amazing grace shone through, and connection led him home.

So I urge all of you—friends, clients, loved ones, and readers—to double down on connection, to place your bets on it.

Connection, and the seven strategies that nourish it, will lead to your true self, inspire others, and help you create the kind of workplace and life that people describe as a game-changer.

Above all, when everything is said and done, it will lead you home.

Call to Action and Resources

Being a Connected Leader is a lifelong process, so stay away (seriously) from quick fixes that promise nirvana in three easy lessons, one powerful webinar, or ten rock-your-world tips. You might pick up valuable and important seeds in these approaches. However, don't think that becoming emotionally whole, spiritually strong, and relationally healthy is a one-time, glad-that's-done project. You are not a project; how could the quality of your life be one?

These are four suggestions I make:

- Read things that inspire, nourish, and help you be the expert of you. In the back of this book are some of my favorite readings that have lifted me up, challenged my thinking, and healed me deeply.
- Develop daily practices that ground you and open you up to the divine wisdom and guidance. Meditation, mindfulness, Centering Prayer, gratitude practices, contemplation, and journaling are a few reflective practices that bring a centeredness to many.
- Create the tribe that elevates your vibe: like-minded people who want similar things from an emotional, spiritual, and relational perspective at work and at home.
- Find guides who will teach you—not only because they are experts in their fields—because they are truly working on their wounds, healing themselves, and are experiencing the process

themselves. So find a clinically-trained coach, a gifted therapist, a wise spiritual director, and/or become part of a twelve-step program to recover from whatever keeps you numb.

I cheer you on as you find work you love and discover ways to transform your leadership so that those around you say, "I'll have what she's having." This is not a DIY initiative, even though at the end, and in the middle, you will learn that you are indeed learning to be alone with yourself, and all of yourself.

In the process of learning to be alone with yourself, you will find the God of your understanding, learn how to reach out to others, and become more of your true self as a result. Interestingly, you will also become an inspiration to others as you dig deep, chase slow, rise up, and become connection walking.

Books I
Connect With

The Art of Possibility: Transforming Professional and Personal Life by Rosamund Stone Zander and Benjamin Zander

Quiet: The Power of Introverts in a World That Can't Stop Talking by Susan Cain

Finding Inner Courage by Mark Nepo

Leadership and Self-Deception: Getting out of the Box by The Arbinger Institute

Real Happiness at Work: Meditations for Accomplishment, Achievement, and Peace by Sharon Salzberg

Big Magic: Creative Living Beyond Fear by Elizabeth Gilbert

Breathing Under Water: Spirituality and the 12 Steps by Richard Rohr

The Return of the Prodigal Son: A Story of Homecoming by Henri J. M. Nouwen

Mindful Work: How Meditation is Changing Business from the Inside Out by David Gelles

Present over Perfect: Leaving Behind Frantic for a Simple, More Soulful Way of Living by Shauna Niequist

Wild at Heart: Discovery the Secret of a Man's Soul by John Eldredge

Almost Everything: Notes on Hope by Anne Lamott

The Road Back to You: An Enneagram Journey to Self-Discovery by Ian Morgan Cron

Fully Human: 3 Steps to Grow Your Emotional Fitness in Work, Leadership, and Life by Susan Packard

Radical Acceptance: Embracing Your Life With the Heart of a Buddha by
    Tara Brach
Broken Open: How Difficult Times Can Help Us Grow by Elizabeth Lesser
Real Love: The Art of Mindful Connection by Sharon Salzberg
Falling Upward: A Spirituality for the Two Halves of Life by Richard Rohr
Joy, Inc.: How We Built a Workplace People Love by Richard Sheridan
Reboot: Leadership and the Art of Growing Up by Jerry Colonna
For the Love by Jen Hatmaker
*Brave Parenting: A Buddhist-Inspired Guide to Raising Emotionally
    Resilient Children* by Krissy Pozatek
Return on Character by Fred Kiel
The Heart Aroused by David Whyte
Let Your Life Speak by Parker Palmer.

Notes

Cover Art Note

1   "Quaking Aspen," The National Wildlife Federation, https://www.nwf.org/Educational-Resources/Wildlife-Guide/Plants-and-Fungi/Quaking-Aspen. Accessed June 14, 2021.

Introduction

2   Leo Nikolayevich Tolstoy, *Pamphlets. Translated from the Russian* (Sydney: Wentworth Press, 2016).

Chapter One

3   Matthew Lieberman, *Social: Why Our Brains Are Wired to Connect* (New York: Broadway Books, 2013), 273.

4   Ian Morgan Cron, *The Road Back To You: An Enneagram Journey to Self-Discovery* (Downers Grove, Illinois: IVP Books an Imprint of InterVarsity Press, 2016), 127.

5   "The Most Accurate and In-Depth Enneagram Report Available," Ianmorgancron.com, https://ianmorgancron.com/assessment. Accessed June 14, 2021.

Chapter Two

[6] Ramus Hougaard and Jacqueline Carter, HBR Emotional Intelligence Series: Mindful Listening. "If You Aspire to be a Great Leader, Be Present," (*Harvard Business Review Press*, 2019), 43.

[7] Susan Packard, *Fully Human: 3 Steps to Grow your Emotional Fitness in Work, Leadership, and Life*. (New York: Tarcher Perigree, 2019), 55.

[8] Rainer Maria Rilke, *Letters to a Young Poet* (New York: Modern Library; Revised ed. Edition, 2001), 44.

[9] Mindful Staff, "Finding Mastery: A Conversation with Michael Gervais and Jewel," *Mindful: Healthy Mind, Healthy Life*, February 9, 2017, https://www.mindful.org/finding-mastery-michael-gervais-jewel/. Accessed June 14, 2021.

Chapter Three

[10] Native American Proverb, origin unknown, frequently cited and attributed just as it is cited here. .

[11] Sue McGreevey, "Eight Weeks to a Better Brain," *The Harvard Gazette*, January 21, 2011, https://news.harvard.edu/gazette/story/2011/01/eight-weeks-to-a-better-brain/. Accessed June 14, 2021.

Chapter Four

[12] Emma Jung and Marie-Louise von Franz, *The Grail Legend* (Princeton, New Jersey: Princeton University Press, 1998), 319.

[13] Theodore Roosevelt, https://www.goodreads.com/quotes/118880-no-one-cares-how-much-you-know-until-they-know. Accessed June 14, 2021.

[14] CS Lewis, *The Four Loves*, (New York: Harper One, an Imprint of HarperCollins Publisher, Originally Published by Harcourt Brace, 1960), 83.

[15] The Reverend John S Nieman, St Margaret's Episcopal Church, Belfast Maine, March 21, 2021.

[16] Jacob Morgan, "The Transformation of Weight Watchers," The Future Organization, last modified February 5, 2018, https://thefutureorganization.com/weight-watchers-transformation/. Accessed June 14, 2021.

17 Joann S. Lublin, "Companies Try a New Strategy: Empathy Training," *The Wall Street Journal*, last modified June 21, 2016, https://www.wsj.com/articles/companies-try-a-new-strategy-empathy-1466501403. Accessed June 14, 2021.

18 "State of Workplace Empathy Report, 2019," Businesssolver.com, 2019, https://info.businessolver.com/empathy-2019-executive-summary. Accessed June 14, 2021.

19 "Microsoft CEO Satya Nadella: How Empathy Sparks Innovation," *Knowledge @ Wharton*, last modified February 22, 2018, http://knowledge.wharton.upenn.edu/article/microsofts-ceo-on-how-empathy-sparks-innovation/. Accessed June 14, 2021.

20 Carolyn Dewar, Scott Keller, Kevin Sneader, and Kurt Strovink, "The CEO moment: Leadership for a new era," McKinsey Insights, July 21, 2020, https://www.mckinsey.com/featured-insights/leadership/the-ceo-moment-leadership-for-a-new-era. July 21, 2020. Accessed June 14, 2021.

21 Zameena Mejia, "Microsoft CEO Satya Nadella attributes his success to this one trait," *CNBC*, last modified February 26, 2018, https://www.cnbc.com/2018/02/26/microsoft-ceo-satya-nadella-attributes-his-success-to-this-one-trait.html. Accessed June 14, 2021.

Chapter Five

22 Sir Ken Robinson, "Do schools kill creativity?," TED Talk, February 2006, https://www.ted.com/talks/ken_robinson_says_schools_kill_creativity?language=en. Accessed June 14, 2021.

23 Albert Einstein, March 11, 1952. Einstein to Carl Seelig, March 11, 1952, AEA 39-013.

24 Brian Grazer and Charles Fishman, *A Curious Mind: The Secret to a Bigger Life* (New York: Simon & Schuster, 2016), 9.

25 Warren Berger, "Why Curious People Are Destined for the C-Suite," *Harvard Business Review*, September 11, 2015, https://hbr.org/2015/09/why-curious-people-are-destined-for-the-c-suite. Accessed June 14, 2021.

26 Emily Campbell, "Six Surprising Benefits of Curiosity," Greater Good Magazine, September 24, 2015, https://greatergood.berkeley.edu/article/item/six_surprising_benefits_of_curiosity. Accessed June 14, 2021.

27 Daniel Siegel, "The Neurobiology of 'We': How Relationships, the Mind, and the Brain Interact to Shape Who We Are," Louisville, Colorado, Sounds True Audio Learning Course, 2008.

Chapter Seven

[28]   Elizabeth Lesser, *Broken Open: How Difficult Times Can Help Us Grow* (New York: Villard Publishers, 2005), 270.

[29]   Rosamund Stone Zander and Benjamin Zander, *The Art of Possibility: Transforming Professional and Personal Life* (London: Penguin Books, 2002), 162.

Chapter Eight

[30]   Parker Palmer, *On the Brink of Everything: Grace, Gravity & Getting Old* (Oakland, CA: Berrett-Koehler Publishers), 27.

[31]   David Whyte, *Consolations: The Solace, Nourishment, and Underlying Meaning of Everyday Words* (Langley, WA: Many Rivers Press, 2015), 50.

[32]   Joseph Campbell, *The Hero with a Thousand Faces* (Novato, CA: New World Library; Third edition; 2008), 18.

[33]   Anne Lamott, *Travelling Mercies: Some Thoughts on Faith* (New York: Anchor Books, 2000), 103.

[34]   Warren Bennis, *On Becoming a Leader* (New York: Basic Books, an Imprint of Hachette Book Group, 2009), xxvii.